THE QUEST FOR TRUTH

Compiled by

Martha Boaz

The Scarecrow Press, Inc.
New York 1961

Dedicated to

ALTHEA WARREN

A Librarian, a warm and loving woman who had a great zest for living and who inspired this volume.

Table of Contents

INTRODUCTION

Wishing to bring authors and students together, the School of Library Science of the University of Southern California, in 1956, started a series of lectures in which outstanding writers were sought out and invited to lecture at the University. The authors were generous in giving copyright permission for their manuscripts and as a result, this volume springs forth full-born, although somewhat slight in size. The range and type of material included is as varied as the mosaic of persons from whom the ideas came. The connecting thread in the lectures is a quest for truth whether it be in a writer's personal and individual search as was true with William Saroyan or in an analysis of the trends of poetry (Stephen Spender and Kenneth Rexroth); fantasy (Robert Nathan); biography (Christopher Herold); books in general (Leonard Wibberley); the minority problem (Leon Uris).

The inspiration for the lecture series and for the subsequent compilation of the manuscripts came from Althea Warren to whom the book is dedicated.

It is the hope of the School that other similar volumes will follow this one.

The Word and the Writer

by

William Saroyan

It is not impossible to imagine this world without a written language, but it *is* useless, for the very weight of books is greater now than the weight of mountains. The Library is larger than the world. Anybody who wishes to do so may stay in the light of the sun as he travels around the world, but a visitor to the library could not, even in a hundred years, travel through more than a small portion of the books there.

There is still only one way to know a book: you must read it.

If a novel such as Huckleberry Finn is made into a movie, it is no longer a novel, it is a movie.

If a musical composition is given the name Leaves of Grass, it is not what Walt Whitman wrote.

If O. Henry's story, The Furnished Room, impelled a designer to achieve a roll of wallpaper, the wallpa-

per would be no more related to the story than if
its theme had been red roses, cherry trees, hatchets, or
the face of Washington as it appears on currency.

A written thing is a written thing.

It must be read in order to be experienced.

In the beginning, the Word was *not*. The Thing was.
The recognition of the thing was visual. The Thing was
itself, and there was no mistake about it. A tree was a tree
as long as it was a tree. It was not a word, spoken or written. An animal was an animal as long as it was. The sun
was the sun, as it still is, whatever its fable and meaning
may be to different people in different places.

But things *look like* other things.

The sea draws pictures on stones, or washes them into
shapes that are not unlike the shapes of bird, animal or
man. Clouds assume forms that seem familiar. The bark
of a tree may contain a picture of a whole countryside.
The wind moving through a tree may make a picture.
The fruit of a tree may resemble any number of other
things. The face of a lion may seem not unlike the face
of somebody's father. The eyes of a calf may seem
as trusting as those of somebody's small daughter.

Everything is specifically itself, but there is nothing
that isn't like something else, if only another of its kind.
At the same time, everything is at least a little unique,
and separate. A grain of sand and another grain of sand
are not the same grain of sand.

The arrival in matter of the Eye may be presumed to
be the beginning of the impulse toward the Word. With
the Eye came Notice, and with Notice came Comparison
and Memory, both of which need help, since things move
so swiftly, change, disappear, die.

The flux of things, the action and change of them,
their rise and decline, blossom and decay, start and stop,
almost *demands* a means by which to arrest this motion,

for purposes of comparison, respect, and study, to name only a few.

If a man killed a bear and wanted everybody to know that he had, he would need to make it clear that he killed a *bear* and not a *beaver*, and that it was *himself* who had killed it. The simplest way to do that is to show the bear and its killer to others. But soon the flesh of the bear is eaten, the bones carved into tools, the skin made into clothing, the killer grows old, and dies. Who remembers that he killed a bear?

There is a sad, an aching need, for man to establish clearly who he is, and what he does. Man believes he is a kind of thing that has meaning, and perhaps even a relationship to something vast and secret and wonderful beyond conception.

Long ago man drew a picture. He made a symbol that stood for himself, and a great many other symbols that stood for other things. For each picture and symbol he had a spoken sound which he could achieve on purpose. Soon he had a whole assortment of pictures and symbols, and sounds and series of sounds.

He had the Word.

He had language, at first only spoken, and then written.

With the Eye and with the Word he made everything, and he's still doing it, although nothing among Things themselves is very much different now than it ever was. He just notices more, and has more to say about everything. The sun, for instance, is still the sun, but the lore about it is now vast, and the relationship of the sun to everything else broadens and enlarges and grows more meaningful every year.

In my opinion, the Word came to pass because Man was both unwilling and unable to believe he was only what he appeared to be: that is, a form of living thing which came into being blindly, and went out of it as blindly as it had come in. For some reason, Man had to have more — more of everything — and so he *made* more.

He made it with the Word.

Why he had to have more, I don't know, and I doubt if anybody else does, or ever has known, but it's certainly something to think about, as of course we've been doing for some time.

That is to say, Man at his *best* had to have more: Man as Man, not as Animal. At less than his best, Man, even now, does not have to have more. What he already has is enough. Great and good multitudes come and go, live and die without demanding, or making more. Such multitudes are constant, and they are not to be considered inferior, or useless, or meaningless. To scorn the multitude, or regret it, would be the equivalent of the Eye scorning the Foot, for Man is Man, and all of him throughout all Mortal Time is One. The Eye sees on behalf of the *Foot*, also. The Founders of the Word, the Users of Language, the Measurers of Less and More, the Creators of Method and Meaning, have done what they have done, and do what they do, for All.

If few write, many read. If few read, many listen, and all speak. Whoever the writer of the Book of Genesis may have been, whatever he may have been thinking at the time, what he wrote belongs to the *multitude, too,* for good or bad, or a little of both. If Genesis isn't altogether Gospel, neither is it entirely Gossip. It certainly isn't Science or History, both of which, though presently highly esteemed, may one day be noticed to have been slightly less than Gospel and only slightly more than Gossip. What the Book of Genesis is is Art. It is Child's Art, even if the writer was an old man, with an old wife, and old children, when he wrote it.

Before the Word, Man wanted more. After the Word,

he wanted also to be Right, or Unmistaken, or at any rate less mistaken then he had been. The Library of the world is full of his joyous and sorrowful seeking after the truth.

As a writer, as one who loves the Word, who is delighted by its buoyant fluidity and angered by its unyielding hardness, I shall not pretend that the following account of my earliest association with the Word, with language, with writing, is common to other writers, or that the account means anything in particular. It means only a little. It's interesting to *me*. And this appears to be an appropriate time to bring it up. It is Gospel in that it's true, and it's Gossip in that it doesn't especially matter that it is true.

I had the good luck of having good eyesight from the beginning. I enjoyed the ability to see, and I delighted in much that I saw. I understood nothing, but nothing hung in the balance on that account, and so it was considered to be enough that I was there, and out of pain.

I did not study how to speak, but I spoke. English first, and later on Armenian, a language *never* spoken by many, and nowadays studied by almost none, and yet a very rich language, which at this moment is beside the point.

When the time came I was sent to public school. It was expected of me that I would soon learn the alphabet, and then that I would learn to read, and then to write.

As it turned out, this actually happened, but the point I want to make is that I remember as vividly as if it were something that was very real only this morning that I saw no reason why it was necesary for me (or for that matter anybody else) to learn to read and write.

I knew how to speak. I could hear. I could see. I could move. And I was getting along fine.

And there, all of a sudden, was something called the

alphabet, and I was expected to understand and use it. I was expected to understand A, and to make something of it. And the same with B, C, D and all the other letters of the alphabet.

Well, to me A was a picture, but I was bullied into believing that it was not a picture; it was A. And so it was with B. I looked at each of the pictures of each of the letters of the alphabet, and I knew which was which, as I knew the sound for each of them. And so in time I knew the alphabet

What I couldn't understand was what good it was, since for years — from what I believed to be the beginning — I had been speaking anyway, without having known the alphabet, without in fact suspecting that speech had anything to do with anything else — without suspecting it had anything to do with words, even. I believed it had to do with me, with love, with family, with house, with world, with human life together in the world. Wasn't that enough? It wasn't. My teacher said it wasn't. My mother said it wasn't. My brother said it wasn't. My sisters said it wasn't. My grandmother who spoke Armenian, Turkish, and Kurdish, but had never gone to school, and who couldn't read or write any language, *also* said it wasn't.

I could breathe and walk and run and eat and sleep and speak and laugh and sing and play and have fun, and even think, so why did I have to read and write, too?

I hated the alphabet. I hated the Word. I hated Language. I knew weeks and months of angry paranoia. I believed unknown parties had devised a diabolic project by which to force me to learn something I didn't want to learn. I was satisfied to be illiterate, to live and look, while everybody else in my class learned to read and write as if it were nothing, as I suspect it *was*. One

morning the teacher printed C, A, T on the blackboard
and asked what the word was. Everybody said cat.
I looked and saw three pictures on the blackboard. Not
one of the pictures, not all *three of them together,* even
remotely resembled a cat. The house in which I lived
had a cat. I knew the cat. I had seen it with a captured
mouse. I had both *seen and heard* it *eat* a mouse. A cat
is alive. It has fur. It speaks, sometimes for a dish of milk,
sometimes just to be speaking. It spreads out near the
stove in the kitchen and sleeps. It wakes up, lifts its head,
and looks around as if it were remembering something.
It gets up on its feet, and it slowly stretches every mus-
cle of its body. It keeps itself clean by licking its fur. It
leaps onto your lap to be nearer than where it had been.
What did C, A, T on the blackboard have to do with
what I knew?

I considered the Word fraudulent. I believed it was
a trick, a deception, a confounder, a liar, a cheat, an in-
timidation, a spoiler of reality, bunk and skulduggery.
All the same, it *had* been established that it was necessary for me to learn to read and write.

I struggled with this problem bitterly. In *thought* I
lived my whole life fully and creatively *without* knowing how to read and write. I planted vines and trees and
harvested grapes and figs. I made kites and flew them. I
met family and friends and spoke with them and loved
them. I whittled things out of wood. I drew pictures on
paper. I made things out of clay. I rode a bicycle back
and forth. I looked at another who also hadn't learned
to read and write and together we smiled at those who
had. I had a house of my own, full of my own kids, who
also didn't know how to read and write, and they were
alive, sensible, and very interesting. In thought, I lived
my whole life without learning to read and write.

Even now, I do not believe I couldn't have lived a full

and creative life without knowing how to read and write. I *could* have, and there's no telling how much more I would have become, or how much more the world, as we say, would have gained.

There is no connection, in other words, between being intelligent and creative and knowing how to read and write.

In time at last I got the hang of it. I learned to read and write. But I don't think we really know what learning is. I didn't *learn* to read and write. If I *had* learned, I would have been reading and writing when everybody else in my class had been doing so, instead of puzzling over the pictures and *pretending* to read, whereas in reality all I was doing was *saying* a whole page which as a *picture* I had come to know signified a series of spoken words. Reading and writing *came* to me. I learned *other things* while I was *supposed* to be learning to read and write. Some of the things I learned are still useful: looking at something *particularly*, for instance, including of course a word on a page. Looking at *the thing* itself, as itself, rather than as the symbol of something else.

My handwriting turned out to be the best not only in my own class, but in the whole school, named Emerson. My letter to Mayor Toomey inviting him to pay the school a visit was judged the best written by any pupil in the school. It was sent to him, and he paid the school a visit.

Before I was eight I began to sell The Fresno Evening Herald after school every day. The newsboys waited for their papers in the basement where the printing press was, and so I witnessed and heard the working of a press as it quickly manufactured hundreds of copies of one day's newspaper. The next day it was a different edition, with different news. I also sold The Saturday Evening Post every Thursday. At home I examined both the newspaper and the magazine, but the Word had not yet come alive for me. *Things only* were alive for me, still.

The Bible figured in the life of my family. I had heard that the Bible was the word of God, and so, naturally, I believed God had written it. It didn't matter that I didn't have a very clear idea as to who or what God was. Without needing to have a clear idea, without needing to define God, I believed I knew who God was, and somewhere along the line I began to believe that not only had He written the Bible, He had written *all* the books. I therefore believed the Word was God's.

I was rather well along in years before the *obviously* true thrust aside the mythical, the marvelous, and in a sense the more deeply true, if superficially false. God, as such, wrote *nothing* as a matter of fact — not the Bible, not the dictionary, not any other book, not even the word cat. *Men* wrote. They wrote the Bible, the dictionary, the books, and cat. Boys, as such, *didn't* write, and for the most part they didn't read, either.

I read around in The Fresno Evening Herald and The Saturday Evening Post, mainly because copies were always around.

Even so, the Word was still away out there somewhere, whether written or read. The book was still away out there. Language was still away out there. I was busy. When I wasn't listenng, I was thinking. What I wanted to know was, what does it mean? In the streets I saw the faces of many people, many *kinds* of them, in all kinds of weather, and under all kinds of circumstances. What did the people mean? What did the world mean?

I didn't know. I didn't know anybody who did. Of if they did, they weren't saying. Or *couldn't*. It was a silent thing. A glace, a half-smile, a slight nod, half a gesture. *That wasn't enough*. I needed to *know*. The earnest faces of the poor, and the smiles of the secure — what did they *mean?* The voices of the anxious and troubled, the shouts of the angry, the cries of the hurt, the whinings of the pitiful, the weeping of the lost and lonely — what did these things mean?

At the First Armenian Presbyterian Sunday School of Fresno one morning I noticed three apple-boxes full of second-hand books on the floor of the hall, and I was invited to take one. I did, and it was trash. It was called Sink or Swim. I read it straight through. It was about a boy who sold papers. Somewhere in the book he sat down and ate bread and butter he had bought with money he had earned.

The reading of Sink or Swim may very well have been the beginning of my life as a writer. It it wasn't, it certainly came very near the beginning. Now, of course, this beginning may be presumed to have been inevitable in any case if we're willing to take our chances here, so that if it hadn't been Sink or Swim, it would have been another book — *any* other. I'm glad it was Sink or Swim, however — trash, that is. Let no one forget the power of *any* book in relation to the right reader at the right time. Let no book be scorned, since *any* book is certainly at least a part of the *one book,* as Donne said of men.

Still, the reading of Sink or Swim didn't bring me understanding, or send me to an examination of all of the books in the Public Library. That was to come later, and again, strictly speaking, unaccountably, or to put it another way, *inevitably,* as part of the unfolding of a whole identity.

I still didn't understand anything, but I was still looking, and still trying.

One day I began to read Oliver Twist by Charles Dickens. In the reading of that preposterous, painful, laughing, sorrowful, eccentric, half-mad, wonderful fable, the

Word moved a little nearer to the center of my spirit, and if I still didn't have any answers, I had a broader order of questions.

Days, weeks, months, and years of watching, waiting, and expecting, and there suddenly in a little story called in English, The Bell, by Guy de Maupassant, I came upon *something* at last. A village beggar with both legs gone swings on his crutches like a gong inside a bell, and so he is called The Bell. The great Frenchman who was himself so much of a child in spite of his superficial worldliness, and so much of a saint in spite of his involvement in what was used to be known as sin, tells the story of the *murder* of the beggar *by neglect* without taking sides, with an *indifference* even, that is soon a rage in the heart and tears in the eyes — not for the beggar, but for life itself, for the whole human race, for the denied and unfortunate, but also for the *undenied* and fortunate, since he and they are one, and the same.

I read this story sometime near the end of my career as a newsboy, a short time before I became a messenger. The immediate effect remained with me the whole afternoon and evening. as I sold papers. I felt that I had got it at last.

This is what it was, and for all I know still is: There is no answer, as such. There is no meaning, as such. All of it must be noticed very carefully, very particularly, and then noticed again. It must be noticed with a clear eye, with love, and with pity.

That day the Word settled down at the center of my spirit. On and off, it has been there ever since.

Sink or Swim. Oliver Twist. A short story by Guy de Maupassant. And one by Jack London, which I read about the same time as I read the story by the Frenchman. Jack London's story was called War.

Perhaps I was a writer from the beginning, in spite of

my childhood quarrel with the whole theory of language.

In any event, these works plunged me headlong into the *working* life of the writer, which begins, as I have said and must say again and again, with careful looking, continues with reading, and begins to be resolved by writing.

What is the purpose of the Word?

In my opinion, its purpose is to influence Man's behavior, nature, and identity *for the better*.

That is not unlike the purpose of the sun in shining on human life, but why should it be? And it doesn't matter that neither the sun nor the Word are able to influence for the better *suddenly*.

I don't remember where I started, or where I wandered, or why, but this is where I stop, for a very simple reason. I've said enough for one time, and I want another try at it, at another time.

Tendencies in Modern Poetry

by

Stephen Spender

When we use the epithet 'modern' in connection with art, we express the thought that there is something unprecedented about the modern world which has created special problems for art.

A great deal of attention has been paid by poets and critics to defining the nature of these problems. So much attention, indeed, that an almost stereotyped picture of what has happened is now accepted, and occurs in literary text books. We read of the break-down of values in industrial civilization, the collapse of communication, the necessity under which poets have laboured to invent symbols and myths as substitutes for the common ground of beliefs and values once shared with the rest of the 'organic community'. The complex picture of the contemporary poet in his isolated and neglected position has become so compelling, that the criticism which portrays it to use, threatens to set up a new kind of prison — the prison of an academy — from which the poet may find it even more difficult to escape than from his once voluntary ivory tower. It will be perhaps a stable rather than an academy: a stable of centaurs each with the head of a new critic attached to the body of a Pegasus.

So we find today young poets, often students of creative writing courses, or else instructors of creative writing courses, with a very conceptualized idea of their role as modern poets. From their practice as poets and their preaching as critics, one gathers that one goes into poetry rather as young diplomats are trained for the foreign service: learning a whole strategy of correct attitudes in order to deal with the various problems that may arise in finding one's way into the anthologies that appear in this difficult modern world. On the other hand, there is also a reaction against this kind of trained poetic diplomacy. Especially in the Bay Area of California, some of the younger poets eschew the intellectual approach. They think of poetry as being a spontaneous outpouring of words resulting from the ecstasy or agony, or both, of existence, stimulated and exacerbated by self-torture, cultivated and added to by drugs, alcohol and orgiastic personal relationships.

It seems to me that poetry today shows very strikingly these two tendencies: the tendency of the academic poet, teaching, learning and writing poems, according to rules and attitudes derived from the study of the practise and ideas of the poets of Eliot's and Pound's generation: and the 'spontaneous' groupings of poets who express a natural reaction — if it is sometimes only the reaction of inferiority complex, — from the academics, and who are probably influenced by remote control from beyond the grave by D. H. Lawrence and Dylan Thomas.

I want to retrace some of the history of these tendencies because I think the current feud is the result of developments during the past thirty years which have had the result of making English and American poetry a kind of special case of literature.

The great crisis of modern poetry was the shock on the sensibility of certain writers caused by the first World War. Historically this might be disputed, because the modern movement anticipated the First World War by a few years. But the war was a catastrophe which cast its shadow before. By the end of the Nineteenth Century, men like Ruskin and Thomas Hardy already had oppressive forebodings of the war cloud hanging over civilization.

The first World War then confronted poets with a situation which disproved the hope, lingering on from the time of Keats, that poetry might create a kind of alternative world of men's imaginings and dreams with an inner strength of intense imagination which will withstand the world of machinery, science and industrialization. Soon after 1914, Death itself lost the tenderness it had for Keats when he whispered that he had been half in love with Death, called it soft names in many a murmured rhyme. The dreamers were driven out of their dreams and put into trenches of the Western Front, where their dreams were not of the stuff which could withstand the horror and the slaughter. Poetry had either to be rejected as being too whimsical, childlike, to withstand this reality, or the imagination had to sup on horror and create a poetry of strength and resilience which could answer the crude language of the modern world with the energy of an inner life that made a new and far more dynamic pattern out of the horrific elements of the external disorder.

In meeting the challenge of the war, two tendencies

are already discernible. I shall call one the innocent, the other the sophisticated.

The innocent was pre-eminently the tendency of those poets who were actually trapped by the fighting and who did not have the time or means to develop sophisticated attitudes. Wilfrid Owen, Siegried Sassoon, Edmund Blunden, Edward Thomas, — all of them for several years in the trenches — were young poets educated in Keats, Shelley and Wordsworth. They were readers doubtless of the anthologies of Georgian poetry, which contained examples of poetry which was the extreme end of the romantic tradition. Confronted by the misery and holocaust of the Western Front the best of the war poets — Wilfred Owen — wrote a kind of poetry which wrenched the Keatsian luxuriant idiom to describe the horror of war. Addressing the young men slaughtered around him in France, the Keatsian sensuousness acquires a ferocious and bitter realism:

Your voice sings not so soft, —
  Though even as wind murmuring through raftered
  loft, —
Your dear voice is not dear,
Gentle, and evening clear,
As theirs whom none now hear
  Now earth has stopped their piteous mouths that
  coughed.

Heart, you were never hot,
  Nor large, nor full like hearts made great with
  shot;
And though your hand be pale,
Paler are all which trail
Your cross through flame and hail;
  Weep, you may weep, for you may touch them not.

How different are the lines I have quoted of Owen from the conceptual tone of Pound and Eliot! This can be seen by comparing Owen with some lines of Ezra Pound, whose subject is also the dead of the First World War:

These fought in any case,
and some believing,
   pro domo, in any case . .
Some quick to arm,
some for adventure,
some from fear of weakness,
some from fear of censure,
some for love of slaughter, in imagination,
learning later . . .
some in fear, learning love of slaughter;
Died some, pro patria,
   non 'dulce' non 'et decor' . . . .

The hard uncompromising bare tone of Ezra Pound seems better suited than that of Owen to the material of the trenches and gunfire. And yet the apparent unsuitability of Owen's Keatsian sensibility involves his Romantic, youthful and above all piteously innocent personality in the sacrifice of the victims in a way that Pound for all his indignation is not involved. One feels in Pound's lines, the poet's superiority and contempt for modern values combined with insight into a tragedy which is that of a botched civilization. For Owen the poetry was in the pity — as he wrote in the preface to his projected volume of poems, and "all a poet can do today is to warn".

The contrast between the innocent of Wilfrid Owen and the much more conscious and sophisticated art of Ezra Pound is significant of two main tendencies in mod-

ern poetry. On the one hand, the immediacy, the involvement, the coincidence of the personally felt experience
with the intensity of expression, of Owen: on the other
hand, the detachment, the objectivity, the studied de-
personalization and impersonality, the use of the actual
experience as an 'occasion' for weaving it into the text-
ure of a mythological view of life and a very deliberate-
ly manipulated language of Pound and Eliot. There is,
of course, no doubt which of the two attitudes has won
the day. Eliot's depersonalizing of poetry, Yeats' elabo-
ration of a constructed mythology providing a system
of reference for his poems, and a storehouse of symbols,
Auden's intellectual grasp of ideologies illustrated
by many of his poems, have produced not only a greatly
respected body of poetry, but also whole libraries of
justifying and elucidating criticism. Intellectual attitudes have won — and perhaps only they could deal
with the complexities of the modern situation. All the
same there has been a constant subterranean revolt
against the intellectual Pegasuses with their heads of
new critics. The tension of modern poetry lies in a conflict between attitudes of innocence and experience.

Side by side with the development of what is certainly today the dominant tendency in poetry, there has
been a far less vocal succession of poets demanding that
poetry should be personal, direct and sincere — a demand that the occasion of a poem should be, in the poet's life one of intensely felt experience forcing its way
into the poetry. Often this feeling goes with a contempt
for literary modes and shared literary aims, and a certain indifference to the technical demands of writing.
This was certainly the case with D. H. Lawrence, who
judged literature chiefly by his feeling that it should express the dynamic purpose of life, and the forces of the
unconscious. It is also of course the view of writers

like Dylan Thomas, George Barker, — and, today, Ginsberg and Kerouac.

Robert Graves is far from being indifferent to technique and the literary vocation, yet — perhaps in part because he endured the experience of the trenches in the first World War — he is extremely suspicious of what he calls the 'synthetic period style'. Graves is outspoken in his criticism of Eliot and Yeats whom he considers (especially Yeats) examples of poets who have inflated their poetry with ideas beyond the compulsion of their poetic experience. Graves writes in a comment on his self-selected poems (in the Anchor book edition): "What readers now want is poems that have been written from a sense of poetic necessity — and with the intention of compressing vital experience into the most economical and lucid form. The mainly negative work begun by the 'modernists' of the Twenties in exploring the limits of technical experiment is finished and done with."

The First World War is a sufficiently removed point from which to consider the schism between two tendencies in modern poetry. For one may take the Western Front as the symptom of the deepest reality, the terrible, which underlies our country. The difference between innocence and sophistication is the difference between being involved in that reality as direct personal experience, and that of viewing it as something external, a problem of history or civilization apprehended as it were at second hand as an overwhelming intellectual problem.

The First World War dramatized the tendency of modern life to confront us with realities so overwhelming that they destroy those who comprehend them — Wilfred Owen — a tendency further exhibited as the methods of Stalin and Hitler — was destroyed by the first World War. The twentieth century has produced evils which seem almost incomprehensible in their anguish and their vastness to those who are outside them, and those who are inside, and in a position to understand, are destroyed. The wars and revolutions, with their by-products of shootings and concentration camps are our own human history.

Apart from these events there is another kind of terribilita of the modern world — the alien universe revealed by science. Modern history and modern science are both 'terrible reality' in their different ways. Each presents the poet with the stark alternative of innocence or experience physically or traumatically entering in and being destroyed by, or standing outside and developing extremely complex attitudes toward the terrible reality. Modern poets are divided into those who experience the modern reality through their own bodies and psyches and those who regard it as a crisis of civilization to be met by an effort of the intellectual will, confronting it with philosophy, or faith, or symbolism, who study to develop attitudes of detachment and irony toward it.

Of course, the two attitudes meet sometimes in the same poet. The poetry of the 1930's was, for example, characterized by an attempt of certain poets to become involved in the events of that period, and to have an objective and detached attitude towards them. Yet the distinction between the poets who intellectualize events and those who are involved in them, remains, I think, true. And it is also true that the dominating influence in poetry from 1920 until the present time, has been of those poets who conceptualized the history which was that of their own time.

The outstanding example of that tendency is, of course, T. S. Eliot. His early work is of a man of most

civilized sensibility who feels that he is living in a period of cultural decline in which people and circumstances — and indeed his own rather ineffective ironi-
cally self-regarded personality — are unpropitious to his
vision of great art which should have found its context
in some different period of history. In *Prufrock* this attitude seems almost an idiosyncrasy, rather like that of
the pre-Raphaelites who romanticized Italian Primi-
tives and who hated the Industrial Nineteenth Century.
The greatness of *The Waste Land* lies in the poet's realization that the crisis was more serious, more general
and more complete than he had thought, and that his
own poetic creativity — his own poetry — was frag-
mented by it. In *The Waste Land* the catastrophe of
western civilization remains a disaster affecting tradition, culture, faith. Yet it was the disaster to civilization
he felt above all, not the murder of millions of human
beings. There is little feeling for the suffering of the victims for the 'hooded hordes swarming/Over endless
plains'. In a world in which values have collapsed there
is no room for pity of mere humanity. In fact, what
Eliot is concerned with is not human suffering, but the
impotence of the intellectual will, the decay of faith. In a
poem which is like a pendant to *The Waste Land, The
Hollow Men,* Eliot's contemporaries are not looked
upon as victims with nerves and hearts, but as 'the hollow men' 'the stuffed men' who have

> Shape without form, shade without colour,
> Paralysed force, gesture without motion.

The poem concludes with the comment that the
world ends 'not with a bang but with a whimper'. Evi-
dently Eliot is thinking here not of a real experience of
the ending of the world but of the experience of the

twittering ghosts of unreal civilization which can only whisper and speak. It is civilization which is ending — has already ended with a whimper, and he does not care about what a younger writer — John Osborne — calls 'the big bang'.

Eliot then sees a war and a post-war world in a very different light from Wilfred Owen witnessing the death of the boys made with teeth for laughing round an apple, and forced to die in the mud of the trenches. For Eliot life is made worth living by the existence of civilizing values, and with the decline of such values men become putrescent nobodies. The only way to meet such a situation is to construct such values as can be pieced together from the fragments of the tradition, to evoke such faith as religion offers to us without distinction of time and place.

Eliot therefore rejects, or disregards, or does not feel, immediate and direct sympathic experience of the human condition around him. He judges the contemporary human condition unworthy by the historic standards of the superhuman or non-human constructions of art and values of the spirit which past civilizations have at times produced. In this he shares with T. E. Hulme, Pound and Yeats, a deliberate rejection of humanism and humanist values. T. E. Hulme outlined an anti-humanistic philosophy which in some ways foreshadows Fascism. The views of Ezra Pound do not require underlining. W. B. Yeats emphasizes again and again in his later poetry his contempt for the mire of human blood, his belief in the super-human works which humanity can only produce through disregard for mere human feelings and sympathies.

Thus the dominating tendency in modern English and American poetry during the past thirty years has been an anti-humanist one. Of course, the anti-humanism is not frivolous. One might defend it by regarding it as a kind of rescuing operation to preserve art from the swamp of destruction, horror, pity and self-pity which has been so great a part of the history of humanity in our times.

All the same, anti-humanist poetry has its limitations and its consequences. There is a price to pay for despising one's contemporaries. Sometimes one feels in Yeats that it is only what Keats — writing of Wordsworth — called the 'egotistical sublime' of the poet which saves his poetry becoming as cold and abstract as the stones of domes and statues he so much admired. The human in Yeats is the poet himself, and a few chosen friends whose lives he has woven into his personal legend. It is interesting that Yeats' father, in his wonderful letters, was always attacking Yeats for his inhumanity. Perhaps because of this, Yeats seems aware in several of his poems of the danger of dehumanization, the heart made a stone by sacrificial politics.

Of course, Eliot never shared the arrogance of Yeats nor the Fascism of Pound, and his poetry is susceptible to expressing moments of sensuous delight in human beings, and of pity. Yet his plays dramatize the extremely narrow bounds of his knowledge of other human beings. His characters represent little more than personified attitudes of acute moral sensibility lost in the Waste Land of the contemporary situation and going out into the world in search of larger enclosing metaphysics or philosophies. To parody the title of a famous play by Pirandello — Six Characters in Search of an Author — they are dramatized poetic monologues in search for a mythology.

The poets of the 1930's, although they were greatly influenced by Eliot and Pound, nevertheless reacted from the ideas of their generation, particularly from their anti-human attitudes. The 1930's was a humanist — and indeed a humane decade — for literature. The effects of anti-humanism were palpably present in the politics of the decade. They had become not theories but active persecutions and were intolerable. Today the poetry of the 1930's is regarded as being political because it was, indeed, affected by the politics of a time in which everybody tended to have a political aspect. Yet W.M. Auden was more of a Freudian psychologist than a Marxist in his poetry. A poet of ideas his ideas were applied to the study of individuals, to an understanding of the complexities of the human heart. Where Eliot's ideas led him to metaphysics, Auden's metaphysics led him back to human beings, and the conclusion of the logic of his poetry is 'We must love one another or die' and 'new styles of architecture, a change of heart'.

Auden is an intellectual poet with an analytic point of view, realizing ideas in brilliant projected images, like a microscope slide projected onto a screen:

Faces along the bar
Cling to their average day:
The lights must never go out,
The music must always play,
All the conventions conspire
To make this fort assume
The furniture of home;
Lest we should see where we are,
Lost in a haunted wood,
Children afraid of the night
Who have never been happy or good.

The windiest militant trash
Important Persons shout
Is not so crude as our wish:

What mad Nijinsky wrote
About Diaghelev
Is true of the normal heart:
For the error bred in the bone
Of each woman and each man
Craves what it cannot have,
Not universal love
But to be loved alone.

This twists beams of christianity, analytic politics and psychology, into a single beam of great power which luminously explores the heart. Auden's achievement here is open, however, to two criticisms which are today made by a younger generation. One is, that Auden uses his undoubted poetic gift of illustrative imagery for a purpose which is not strictly poetic, namely to analyse, elucidate, explain. His poetry lends brightness and vividness to didactic ideas, it does not lead through the ideas into a world where the poetry becomes the end of the journey, an end in itself. The second criticism is that Auden stands outside his own poetry. He remains as it were a didactic figure in the laboratory using his poetic instruments to produce his diagrammatic results but not committed with his whole personality to these results, indeed singularly uncommitted. Even when he writes as a christian there is very little of the believing converted Auden in his poetry. He seems rather to be offering christianity as as ideology which is an improved version of Marx and Freud, nearer to the truths he has observed about men and women, than the theses of socialist politics or Freudian analysis. It is difficult for the reader to feel convinced by the faith of a person who seems curiously detached from his own conversion.

The movement in poetry which began already in the 1930's with Dylan Thomas represents a reaction from

the intellectualism and anti-humanism of Eliot, and the
non-involvement in his own personality of Auden. When
I say that it is a 'reaction', I am using that word in a
general sense to imply the change of attitude and personality which the reader of Eliot and Auden would feel
when he read Dylan Thomas. I do not mean that Thomas
set himself up to oppose older poets whom he evident-
ly admired. When I speak of a movement which began
with Thomas, I am not thinking of some literary racket like the New Apocalyptics who were known for a few
months at the end of the Second World War as a self-
propaganding literary Movement. I mean that Thomas
expressed something which Eliot was too inhibited to
realize in his poetry, Auden too intellectually detached,
and which corresponded to a need in poetry which readers and younger poets have felt and still feel. There is a
great deal of Freudian psychological material in Thomas, but where, in Auden this would lead back through
poetry, into intellectual analysis, in Thomas the tangled
complexes of the poet lost in his own childhood, his own
sexuality, leads into a forest which is pure poetry. And
since it is poetry he does not try to get out of the forest.

Light breaks where no sun shines;
Where no sea runs, the waters of the heart
Push in their tides;
And, broken ghosts with glowworms in their heads,
The things of light
File through the flesh where no flesh decks the bones.

A candle in the thighs
Warms youth and seed and burns the seeds of age;
Where no seed stirs,
The fruit of man unwrinkles in the stars,
Bright as a fig;

Where no wax is, the candle shows its hairs.

In this, Dylan Thomas returns to the horrified innocence of Wilfred Owen, completely involved in his
own reactions to the mud and blood and mire of life
which for Owen was the Western Front, for Thomas,
his involvement in the wonder and horror of his childhood and adolescent body; the death from cancer of
his father. Perhaps a hundred years hence literary historians will consider that a cycle in English and American poetry came full circle with Dylan Thomas. It began with the somewhat neglected poetry of the first
World War, the poetry of innocence of Wilfred Owen.
It continued with the rejection of the terrible involvement in humanity of the war poets and the attempt to
submit belief in humanity, pity for humanity, hope for
humanity — to theocratic or aristocratic systematiza-
tions which we find in Eliot, Pound and Yeats, the attempt to analyze men and women and use poetry as a
means of reconciling them through Marxist, Freudian
and christian ideology of Auden. It comes full circle
with the return to desperate pitiable wholly accepted
and poetic human individuality of Dylan Thomas.

There is then a very broad division of tendencies in
modern poetry: the division of innocence and experience. The innocents tend to identify themselves with
victims, and to return to situations which are those of
childhood. The experienced tend to make a heroic effort to attain a maturity which puts them on the side of
a tradition which they themselves believe to have no
roots in modern life. In the attempt to form a poetic
philosophy which is a post mortem on the whole of past
western civilization, they are prepared to throw out contemporary humanity.

Of course, a good many poets stand midway between

both tendencies, as does, no doubt, Auden. Moreover, throughout the whole of the period of which I have been talking, there were considerable poets — Robert Frost, Robert Graves, D. H. Lawrence — who, for different reasons, never accepted the domination of Eliot and Pound and the immense machinery of modern criticism to which their ideas gave rise.

Deeper issues than the comparatively surface ones of poets reacting against one another are involved in the feud of innocence versus experience. One of these is the relation of poetry to the values of a world where science and progress have largely replaced traditional beliefs. Science alters the scale of existence, so that man, measuring himself against immensities, feels his infinitesimally small point in time and space almost obliterated by the external reality. Progress has the effect of constantly shifting the meanings of words and values, introducing new factors into the environment which make it extremely difficult to construct a poetic symbolism. Philosophy, in undermining the meanings of words employed in metaphysics and morals, has undermined language itself.

Thus it is understandable that poets should think they stand in the greatest need of all the support they can get for the constructions of their poetry from external structures of thought whether these survive in traditions, can be conjured up by faith, or are supplied by political or psychological ideologies. More important still, language has never stood in greater need of literature to rescue it from the corruption of commercial and propagandist uses, confusion of values, the imprecise abstractions and generalizations of psychologists and sociologists, than it does now. Perhaps the greatest claim one can make for the poetry of Eliot and Pound is that it is a scrupulous and precise use of language, and the hardest criticism of Dylan Thomas of his later followers, that he and they are often neglectful of the intellectual quality of language.

Thus on the side of the poets of experience it may be said that there is an objective task of modern poetry — to redeem language by using words with the same precision as scientists define formulae, to invent contexts of imagined situations in which the words undermined by analytic philosophy are still connected to their traditional meanings. The great achievement of the generation of Eliot and Pound is that in liberating poetry from the habits and modes of post-Victorian poeticization they have constructed forms in which words can be used with the utmost precision.

All the same, there is the danger that having done this, poetry in rescuing language, is in danger of becoming a machinery for inventing contexts illustrating the dictionary uses of a new academicism. The followers of Eliot and Empson who write a correct verbally conscious, technically appropriate, poetry of ideas, without their having Eliot's sensibility and tragic awareness of the state of civilization, are open to this charge. One can understand why the young react violently against the new academic poets and go in pursuit of their personalities, which they hope will prove to be demonic. The writers who practise what Graves calls the 'synthetic period style' — the style which contains myths in the manner of Yeats, ambiguities in the manner of Empson, references in the manner of Eliot, and conscious influences in the manner of Auden, produce an inevitable reaction against their thinness and lack of vitality.

It is inevitable that there should be a conscious reaction against any developments which seem to point to new academicism, and that the reaction should take the form of expressing personal emotions with the greatest violence and without much regard for words or form, fighting an over-intellectual kind of poetry with an incantatory kind of poetry, passionate subjectivity against dispassionate objectivity. Dylan Thomas and his later followers are driven to ever greater extremes of self-maceration in order to create a dynamism of their personalities which confronts the age of impersonality. If they remind us sometimes of moths hurling themselves into life as into a flame and falling to the ground with wings burnt, then we ought to reflect that unless our objectivity and our intellectual effort can make as great an affirmation, then they mean considerably less than any assertion of real living, however futile this may seem.

And in fact the alternation from passionate subjectivity to an extremely lucid flame-like objectivity seems almost inevitable in our time. These are the two alternative paths — that of innocence and that of experience — one of which the poet today has to choose.

The Democratic Revolution

by

Mortimer Adler

INTRODUCTION

This century has witnessed, is still witnessing, and I hope will continue to witness, one of the greatest revolutions that has taken place since the emergence of civilization itself. Using Arnold Toynbee as my guide, I would date the beginning of civilization at six thousand years ago. The only revolutions in the past which are as important as the democratic revolution in our century, are the one which saw the rise of cities, and the one when cities first became republics. Since the first, which started six thousand years ago and the second, which occurred about twenty-five hundred years ago the revolution that I want to talk about in this lecture is the only great revolution that has taken place in human affairs.

Let me mention one other thing that Arnold Toynbee

says in the light of his study of the twenty-five or twenty-six civilizations which once existed, most of which have now disappeared. He tells us that two evils destroyed most of them. These are the twin evils of *class* and *war*.

The democratic revolution may remove from human life one of these evils — the evil of class. We will then still have the evil of war to deal with. It may take a fourth, and greatest revolution of them all, to cure that evil.

Revolution as a Term of Praise

I have used the word "revolution" as a term of praise. Many people use the word "revolution" for something to be feared, and use the word "revolutionist" as a term of derogation. The word has many meanings. It means a radical change, *with* violence or *without* violence; and a change which can be *progressive* or *retrogressive*. All of these possibilities fall within the meaning of the term. But I would not be using it as a term of praise except to connote a progressive change that is accomplished, for the most part, without violence. The revolution that I am talking about is a non-violent revolution and progressive.

It is important to recognize this because it helps us to understand that the United States is, in the best sense, the most revolutionary of countries. I share this opinion, by the way, with the editors of *Fortune*. The editors of *Fortune*, some years ago, devoted an entire issue to one article, which they later published as a book, entitled "U.S.A. — A Permanent Revolution." What they tried to express in that title was simply that the traditions of our country are revolutionary throughout.

The History and Theory of This Revolution

Since we are concerned with the democratic revolution as a *progressive* change, we have to be concerned with the *theory* of the matter as well as the *history* of it. History, by itself, will not support a judgment of progress. You can report, historically, that such changes have taken place. You can also narrate what changes are taking place. But in order to say that the changes are in the line of progress, it is necessary to say that the change is from worse to better. In order to say that things are getting better, you must have some principles or standards of measurement. Hence I must begin with the basic theory of democracy and tell you, as quickly and simply as I can, *what democracy is* and *why it is the political ideal.* When I say "the political ideal," I mean the *only* just, or the *most perfectly and completely* just, form of government, or political organization.

If you ask most Americans what democracy is, they are not able to give you a clear or precise definition of it. If you ask them why they are for democracy, they are not able to give you the reasons which demonstrate its goodness. They are for it without knowing very much about what it is, or why it is good. This seems to be a very bad state of affairs. If we are dedicated to democracy, we had better understand what it is and why it is good.

After I have stated the theory of democracy, I would like to have you look at the sweep of the last three thousand years on a large canvas, because I want you to see what stages of progress have brought us to the point at which the democratic revolution starts. Many changes have prepared the way for it. But the revolution itself began only toward the end of the last century. It is as recent as that and is by no means completed.

The fact that the democratic revolution began only yesterday is very important for everyone to understand. I was taught in school — and I am sure most children are still taught in school — that this country was founded as a democracy. That is completely false. No one in the eighteenth century understood democracy very clearly, and what they understood they did not like. No eighteenth century government was a democracy.

Finally, I want to ask how far we have progressed in the democratic revolution and what remains to be done, what obstacles must be overcome. I shall leave to you the question of our prospects of overcoming these obstacles.

THE THEORY OF DEMOCRACY: DEFINITION AND DEMONSTRATION

Let me start with an analysis of the forms of government. This will enable you to see what democracy is, and why it is the only just, or the only completely just, form of government. Let me ask you to think of the following relationships.

Three Possible Relations Between Men as Rulers and Ruled

Government is a relation that involves ruler and ruled. It happens in the family: parents rule children. It happens in the factory when men manage machines. All these words — "manage," "control," "direct," "rule" — connote government.

Man as ruler is related to three different types of objects — that which he rules. The object he rules is either a thing or a person. And when persons are ruled, they are either mature or immature. They are either children or adults.

Let us look at these three for a moment. How should a man rule things: for their own good, or for man's good? The answer is, *for the human good.* We manage machines, we direct and control animals, for our good. We do not do it for the good of the machine, or for the good of the animal. This is quite proper, because of the radical inequality that exists between men and things, or persons and things. How should parents rule children? For the parents' good or for the child's good? You know the answer to that. A proper parent, understanding his duties and his vocation, rules the child for the child's good, so long as the child remains a child.

When you are ruling a thing, you do not consult the thing. You do not consult the machine about how it wants to be governed; you do not seek its consent to government, nor grant it participation in government. When a child is very young, you rule it in the same way. You do not ask the child's consent to being ruled. You do not ask the child's opinion in reaching decisions on family matters. The child is ruled *absolutely*, in the sense of *without participation*, yet *for the child's good*.

Finally, we come to the case in which man rules man, both being adult. As in the case of the child, the rule should be for the good of the ruled. But now, because of the equality among all mature persons, the rule should not be absolute, but with consent on the part of the ruled and with his participation in government.

From these three relationships, you can see at once two ways in which men can be misrruled. When men are ruled as if they were things, i.e., *ruled or governed for the good of the ruler, with no voice in their own government*, ruler and ruled are related as tyrant and slave. Men ruled as slaves are men being used as instruments and so being misused, because they are persons being treated as if they were things. And when one man rules another paternalistically as if that other were a child, the rule is despotic. In fact, the Greek word "despotic" actually means the rule of *paterfamilias*, the rule of the householder over the immature persons in the family. When such rule is over children, it is not a bad rule; but when this kind of rule is exercised over mature persons,

they are subjected to despotism, even if they are benevolently ruled

The only just or proper rule of one person over another
is one in which they are related as equals, and both have
a voice in their common affairs, though they may have
different functions. Let me illustrate this.

The first distinction among the forms of government
is the distinction between tyranny and all the other
forms. Tyranny, we can say, is absolutely unjust. What
we mean by tyranny is that kind of government in which
men are treated as things and so are enslaved.

The second basic distinction is more important, but a
little harder to understand. It is the distinction between
absolute and *limited* government; or, if you will, between
a *government of men* and a *government of laws*. Limited
government, republican government, constitutional government, government of laws, are all ways of saying the
same thing. On the other hand, there is absolute government, despotic government, government of men.

The most interesting way of expressing the distinction
is in terms of *government of laws* and *government of
men*. You may think it is absurd to contrast government
of laws and government of men. Every government involves laws or regulations, and men are always also involved. Of course, but that is not the meaning of the
distinction. What then *is* meant when we say: "Ours is a
government of laws, not men." We mean that the rulers
do not rule by any power or authority vested in their own
persons. We mean that the rulers rule only as office-holders, by virtue of such power or authority as is vested in
the office they hold; and this office is limited by the fundamental law of the land — the constitution. That is why
we say it is limited government. The power office-holders can exercise is limited by the office they hold. They
wield it only as long as they hold the office. More-

over, they can be thrown out of office for misuse of it. Above all, in this form of government, the most important office is that of citizenship.

Citizenship

If you were to ask "What is the basic office that anyone can hold in a republican or constitutional form of government?" I would not say "the presidency" or the "chief magistracy." I would say "citizenship." For that is the only permanent office and the one that is prerequisite to holding any other.

This is of the utmost importance to understand. If you understand that a constitutional government is rule by office-holders, and that they rule citizens who are their equals, citizens who have a voice in electing them and a voice in the government which they administer, you see that constitutional government is government of, by, and for citizens. Such government is a government of free men and equals who rule and are ruled in turn. It is quite different from despotic government, in which those who are ruled have no voice in their own affairs. They are not ruled as equals, but by a "superior" man who rules them benevolently and takes care of them.

Once you set up constitutional government, and with it the office of citizenship, the question arises: *Who shall be citizens?* Some men, or all? If some, which? This is the great question that any constitutional government must face as soon as it exists.

Grounds for Exclusion from Citizenship

There are only three just grounds for excluding anyone from citizenship. They are: *infancy, mental deficiency* (any of the insanities or feeble-minded conditions) and *criminal turpitude.* No other attribute of man justly disqualifies him from citizenship. If I am right about this, then a just constitution is built upon the principle of universal suffrage; and an unjust constitution is a constitution that has *restricted franchise*.

"Suffrage" and "Franchise"

Within the large genus of republics, or constitutional governments, there is now a third and final distinction among the forms of government. Any republic or constitutional government with a restricted franchise, with restrictions other than the three disqualifications I have just mentioned, is an *oligarchy*. A constitution in which you have universal suffrage, with no more than the three disqualifications mentioned, is a *democracy*.

The democratic principle of suffrage is *universal and equal* manhood suffrage — one man, one vote. This defines democracy. Democracy is *republican or constitutional government, in the constitution of which is embodied the principle of universal, equal manhood suffrage. It is, therefore a politically classless society with equal rights and liberties for all.* There are no unjustly disfranchised persons. Or, in the language of John Stuart Mill, there are no "political pariahs." No one is disqualified except by his own default.

Equality and Liberty

I would like to call your attention to this last point. The two words "equality" and "liberty" are great words to conjure up all kinds of fundamental notions; and we are often torn between what they imply. The institution of republican government is, in the first instance, a great step forward toward *liberty*. Until you have republican government, no one is free. Under tyrannies or despotisms, the ruled are always subjected or enslaved. The transition from absolute, despotic, and tyrannical governments to republics is the transition from *no* freedom to *some* freedom. The other transition, from oligarchical republics to democratic republics, is not a transition from no freedom to some freedom. It is a transition from *freedom for some men* to *freedom for all men*. In other words, the democratic revolution, the democratic change, is governed by the principle of equality, as the republican change is governed by the principle of *liberty*.

The great thing that came into the world with the establishment of republics is freedom. The great thing that came into the world with the establishment of democracy is equality. That is why I do not refer to democracy as *the free society*. That it is free goes without saying. But freedom is only part of the picture. Freedom exists in republics that are not democratic. The essence of democracy is equal freedom for all. And that is why a democracy is most accurately described as a politically classless society.

Three Principles of Democracy

Having defined democracy, let me now try to demonstrate that it is the ideal, the most just or the only perfectly just form of government. This truth rests on three principles. If these three principles are true, the conclusion about democracy is sound. The three principles are as follows.

(1) *Man is by nature a political animal*. All men are by nature *constitutional* animals. Let me explain. We are gregarious; we need to associate with our fellowmen. Many other animals are gregarious also: the social insects (wasps, ants, termites) and the herding mammals (elephants, wolves, and bison). But we differ from all the other herding or gregarious animals by the fact that they associate by instinct. The forms of their association are fixed by their very nature. We do not associate by in-

stinct. We associate by need; and when we associate, we do so by reason and free will. That is why, if you look at human associations — the family or tribe, the city or state — you see the wide variety of forms that human association takes. We *constitute* them ourselves. That is what I mean by saying "man is by nature a political or constitutional animal."

(2) My second proposition is one that I take from the Declaration of Independence: *All men are by nature equal*. I do not mean that they are all equally strong, equally bright, equally charming, equally anything else *except one thing*. They are all equally persons, and the most important thing I can say about a person is that *all persons are of equal worth*. One person is not worth more than another. The intrinsic dignity and worth of all persons is the same.

(3) The third principle of this demonstration is the principle of justice, which is, simply, that *we should treat equals equally and unequals unequally*. Since all men are equal as persons, you can see the absolute injustice of tyranny, in which men are treated as things; the slight justice of benevolent despotism, in which men are treated as persons, but treated as unequals, as children rather than as men; the relatively greater justice of oligarchical government, in which *some men*, at least, are treated as full equals; and finally, the absolute and perfect justice of democracy, in which all men are treated as they should be treated namely, as persons, as political animals, and as full equals.

I said that justice requires us to treat equals equally and unequals unequally. You may ask, therefore: What about human inequalities? In view of the fact that men are both equal and unequal, should not the inequality of men be recognized politically?

Egalitarian Democracy and Aristocracy

The answer is "Yes." We must avoid two false extremes. One is egalitarian democracy, which considers only the equality of men and pays no attention to their inequality. In some of the Greek city-states, for example, the magistrates were chosen by lot from the citizenry on the ground that all were equally capable of holding any public office. They made no effort to select superior men for superior offices in the state. This is wrong. A democracy should recognize that there is a hierarchy of functions to be performed and a hierarchy of men to perform them. Such recognition of a hierarchy of functions and of capacities acknowledges human inequality in a way that is not inconsistent with the fundamental principle of democratic equality.

On the other hand, an aristocracy of fixed or hereditary classes, which is usually a masked oligarchy, gives some men special privileges and powers without regard to merit on their part. We must observe here the distinction made by Thomas Jefferson in his correspondence with John Adams about aristocracy. Jefferson distinguished between the artificial aristocracies of specially privileged classes and the natural aristocracy—the aristocracy of talent or virtue. Jefferson thought that a natural aristocracy was the most important ingredient in any society.

Applying Jefferson's insight, we can now define democracy as a politically classless society with a rotating aristocracy. Each generation has its own aristocracy, and no aristocracy that reaches the top in that generation perpetuates itself into the next. Each generation produces its own best men to perform the most important functions of government.

HISTORY OF THE MOTION
TOWARD DEMOCRACY

Now let us look at the history of the progress toward democracy. Let me divide the history into two stages. The first stage runs from the sixth century B.C. to the nineteenth century; the second stage, from the middle of the nineteenth century to the present day.

The First Stage

The first stage is the story of the first great political revolution — the revolution which sets up constitutional government.

The first cities were under royal rule, under despotic rule. Why? Because they actually grew out of families and tribes. Cities like Athens and Rome were nothing but amalgamations of small groups or tribes that came to live together. Since, in the family or tribe, the rule of the elders prevailed, paternal or royal rule was simply a perpetuation of the rule of the old men of the tribe. But, says Aristotle, the man who first founded the state was the greatest of benefactors. A more accurate translation of the Greek would be "the man who first *constituted* the state was the greatest of benefactors." Aristotle thus celebrates the genius who first saw that it was possible for men to live in cities without paternal or royal rule, and under a constitution. The invention of constitutional government took place around the fifth century B.C. It was an invention more far-reaching and important than any of the mechanical inventions of our industrial life.

The first republics — Athens, Sparta, Thebes, and Corinth — were puny as compared with the great empires of Persia and Egypt. As tyrants and despots so often feel, the Persian king could not stand having these small groups of free men living in his vicinity. This finally led to the Persian attack on Greece. The Greeks, a handful

of them, in the mountain passes at Thermopoli, on the
plains, and on the sea, beat the Persians back. We always
look upon this as a great victory of free men over slaves.
It was a magnificent victory. Constitutional government
defended itself and triumphed. How long did that
triumph last? How long did these Greek cities endure?
Less than one hundred years. Why did they collapse?
Two reasons:

1. They were internally torn by class divisions. What
Karl Marx calls the class war is described by Plato and
Aristotle as "the conflict between the city of the rich and
the city of the poor." Quite apart from the slave revolts
in Sparta, the fight between the rich and the poor in all
the Greek cities was one of the causes of their down-fall.

2. The other cause was external war. The imperialism
of Athens and Sparta brought on the Peloponnesian
war, and so weakened these cities that Philip of Macedon
could sweep down from the north and conquer them. In
less than one hundred years there was not a trace of
republican or constitutional government left on the face
of the earth. Less than a hundred years!

After the fall of Rome, Europe was splintered by the
feudal system. There were thousands of small principali-
ties, duchies, counties—small earls and petty lord, each
with his own little domain. Slowly, out of this anarchy
the medieval kingdom developed. It was quite different
from the kingdoms of antiquity.

The medieval king, under the feudal system, had a
contractual relation with the nobles of his realm. I want
to read to you the language in which the nobles of
Aragon expressed their pledge of fealty to the king, at
the same time that he swore his coronation oath before
them. "We who are as good as you, swear to you,who are
no better than we, to accept you as our King, provided
you observe all our liberties and laws; but if not, not."

Thus we see that the king was not an absolute ruler, but was bound by constitutional limitations. When King John was made to sign Magna Carta by the nobles, the constitution was being enforced. How long did such government last? Not much beyond the fifteenth century. After that you have the emergence of the Hapsburgs in Austria, Spain and the Low Countries; the Tudors and the Stuarts in England; and finally, the Bourbons in France. These kings dissolved the royal and political regime by throwing its constitutional aspect out, and making the government purely royal. By the time you get to the sixteenth and seventeenth centuries, there is no vestige of constitutional government in Europe. Kingdoms were again as despotic as they had been in antiquity.

What happens next? The republican revolution takes place once again in the seventeenth and eighteenth centuries: the great revolution in England in 1688, which threw the Stuarts out and brought in the Prince of Orange; the American revolution of 1776; the French revolution of 1789. This continues through the nineteenth century: in Middle Europe, in 1848; in South America, where republics emerge in the middle of the nineteenth century; right down to 1905, when Russia had its first revolution and the people obtained a parliament from the Czar.

From 1688 to 1905, a revolution was going on in the western world. What kind of revolution? A democratic revolution? Not at all! The republican revolution, the same one that the Greeks started. It has taken place again and again. And that revolution is still far from established. In our own lifetime, it has been lost in Germany, Italy, Spain, and Argentina. Do not think, therefore, that the republican revolution is an assured success. It is still something we have to preserve, because without *republi-*

can institutions, *democracies* cannot come into being. But republican institutions are not democracies; they are the precursors of them.

The Second Stage

I turn now to the second stage, which has taken place within the last 150 years. Let me divide my story into two parts: first, what happened in the world of action; and second, what happened in the world of thought.

If I were forced to put my finger on a point in history, a time and place of which I could say "Here in the world of action, the stirrings toward democracy first showed themselves," I would put my finger on the dateline of 1647. At that time, on a field in Putney, England, in the midst of Cromwell's army, a group of men called the Levellers, led by Major Rainborough and Sir John Wildman told Cromwell and Colonel Ireton (his son-in-law) what they wanted when the war against King Charles was won. They said, "We would like to know, after we have this war against the King, who are going to be the *people* of England?"

That is quite a question, isn't it? "Who are going to be the *people* of England?" Rainborough and Wildman took the position that "every he who breathes the air of England has as much interest in this land, and as much right to have a voice in his own government as the richest he among us." Ireton and Cromwell said No to this demand; for they felt that if every man had an equal voice in the affairs of England, then those with a fixed and permanent interest in landed estates and commercial ventures patented by the King would soon be voted out of their property, they believed it was necessary to restrict suffrage to the men of property. This seemed a reasonable position at the time. If you gave every man an equal voice, the poor would dominate Parliament and it would not be long before they would find a way to change the property relationships.

In 1789, our forefathers met in Philadelphia for two years to debate the framework of our Constitution. The question of suffrage was raised, but no one spoke out for universal suffrage. They could not agree about the precise extent to which suffrage should be restricted. They left this matter to the separate states.

In New York State, in 1821, there was a convention to reform the Constitution of New York. It was called for the purpose of broadening the suffrage. Before 1821, only farmers in upstate New York with a freehold of five hundred pounds a year elected the Senators of the Upper House. The people with less property than that could vote only for the Assembly. The proposed reform was to enable everyone to vote for Senators as well as for Assemblymen.

Chancellor Kent, one of the great legal figures in New York State, speaking against this in 1821, said exactly what Ireton and Cromwell had said: "This mania for universal suffrage jeopardizes the principles of property and the principles of liberty." That it jeopardizes the principles of property is perfectly clear; that it jeopardizes the principles of liberty is not so clear. The only liberty that is threatened is the greater freedom of the rich as against the poor. Equal suffrage would make their freedom equal.

In England, the three great reform bills of the 1830s, 1860s, and 1880s — and finally the House of Lords Act in 1911—were required to bring about the constitutional changes by which the English form of government approached democracy. Even then, the Women's Suffrage Act, which enfranchised one-half of the population, did not take effect until 1918 in England.

In this country, there were no suffrage reforms in the Jacksonian period. We talk about Jacksonian democracy; but during the period of Jackson and for ten or fifteen years afterward there were men in this country who carried ball-and-chain and were indentured servants. There was a vast, disfranchised horde of those who may have had some *protection* from the state, but certainly had no *privileges* in the state — no voice in their own government. The Civil War amendments began to change the picture, but you have to wait until 1920 in this country before the female half of the population is enfranchised. This indicates how very recent democracy is in the two most advanced countries in the world.

Let us look now at the realm of political thought. When did political philosophers first come to regard democracy as ideal? No thinker prior to 1800 had ever spoken a good word for democracy. In the vast literature of political theory, there are no proponents of democracy prior to 1800. With the possible exception of Robert Owen, the first voice that speaks for democracy is raised in 1835. It is the voice of a Frenchman, Alexis De Tocqueville, who came to this country and wrote a book—not for Americans, but for Europeans to read—called "Democracy in America." I cannot recommend any book more highly. It is not only an amazing journal of observation, but an amazing book of prophecy. De Tocqueville, in effect, said: "For the first time in the history of mankind, a people is beginning to experience equality of conditions. America is setting up a society in which, eventually, equality of conditions will prevail." This is what he meant by democracy, and quite rightly. And he said to his European brethren: "This revolution, once started, will never stop. It may be misguided, it may have abuses, it may fall short of its own great destiny, but it will never be stopped. It will sweep the world."

De Tocqueville's work was not, however, a great work in political theory. The first great book of political theory which holds democracy up as the ideal is dated 1863. It is John Stuart Mill's "Representative Government." Even so, John Stuart Mill, like many of us today, was a reluctant democrat. He wanted universal suffrage, but he also wanted it unequal. He wanted to give the brighter people, the technically more advanced people, more votes than the rest. He could not bring himself to trust the laboring classes in 1863. Yet he spoke out for women's suffrage. All in all, Mill represents the first advocate of universal suffrage among the great political philosophers.

THE DEMOCRATIC REVOLUTION IN PROCESS — HOW FAR IT HAS SUCCEEDED

Let me first ask why it took so long to get started? Why, if democracy is the ideal, did it take so long for men to recognize it? The answer, I think, is not that men are obtuse or blind to the truth; it is not that men are intrinsically unjust or hard-hearted. None of these things is the answer. The answer is that no one could see the truth prior to industrialization. That is why we are absolutely wrong if we think we can carry democracy to India or China today, to the Middle East or Middle Europe. In no place where industrialization is not yet advanced can democracy either exist or be understood.

I will have more to say about this in my next lecture. Industrialization brings about an indispensable emancipation of men, which makes democracy possible in fact and thinkable to the mind. This explains why most of the world, which is still at a low level of industrialization, is still not ready to think or act democratically.

Now the question we must face is, does democracy

fully exist anywhere, even on paper? I know it does not exist in England and the United States. It may exist in Switzerland, the Scandinavian countries, Canada, Australia, or New Zealand. In England, even though the House of Lords is just a vestige of its former self, even though the Lords are almost shorn of power, nevertheless, the existence of the House of Lords, constitutionally, is undemocratic. And in our country, the poll tax, which operates against universal suffrage, must be abolished from every state by an amendment to the federal constitution.

But even if these changes took place—even if we had the poll tax amendment ratified and in operation—would America be a democracy, a working democracy, a democracy in social fact and actual practice? Anyone who reads the daily newspapers knows the answer.

Democracy has three major obstacles to overcome. The first is that conditions of equality must be more than conditions of political equality; they must be conditions of economic equality, too. Economic democracy is needed for political democracy.

Secondly, conditions of equality require equal educational opportunity for all. That does not mean an equal number of years in school for all. It means that the *best* education, the education once given to the few, must now be given to all.

Until these problems are solved, the democratic revolution will not be completed. It may take us at least one hundred years to solve them.

The third obstacle to the prosperity and completion of the democratic revolution is the one that Arnold Toynbee mentioned — the evil of war. Even if we remove the evil of class, we still have to face the evil of war.

War consumes too much of our wealth. Democratic education and economic democracy require us to make a better use of wealth. But this is only part of the reason why war threatens democracy. The other is the one that Alexander Hamilton states so succinctly in *The Federalist Papers*. Let me read you what he said: "The violent destruction of life and property, incident to war, the continual effort and alarm attendant on a state of continual danger, will compel nations the most attached to liberty to resort for repose and security to institutions which have a tendency to destroy their civil and political rights. To be more safe, they at length become willing to run the risk of being less free."

We know this to be true in our own day. The threat of war is inimicable to the best interests of democracy. Liberty, justice, rights, cannot be preserved in a state of war — the cold war which we have suffered so long. Democracy needs world peace in which to develop and prosper.

The Biographer at Work

by

Christopher Herold

From the various topics Miss Boaz kindly suggested for my talk today, I selected "The Biographer at Work." I was given ample time to meditate on this subject; but it unfortunately so happens that this particular biographer, when at work, is faced with one problem that overshadows all others: he hates work. To overcome this tragic handicap, nothing will serve except a firm deadline, which he has a tendency to forget for as long as possible. I confess that I never really begin work until there is hardly a minute to spare, and this goes not only for writing biographies but also for lectures.

I shall not say how close to the deadline it was when I began to think in a more or less sustained manner about what I was to say today. Somewhat to my horror, I discovered an odd thing. For indeed it does seem odd that someone whose reputation, what little there is of it, rests

on having written a biography, should never, until a
few days ago, have given any thought to the problems
of biography in general. Naturally, I gave a great deal
of thought to the particular problems that faced
me when I was working on a particular biography.
I cannot say that I am a very avid reader of biographies;
and I have never read a book on how to write biography.
I am simply a fool who treads where angels are more
cautious. If I had given much thought to the writing of
biography before I wrote one, I probably would never
have written any, and you may be sure that I'll think
twice before I write another. For writing the life of another is at bottom an impertinent, hopeless, and exceedingly laborious enterprise that leaves one, in the end,
with a sense of failure.

Although biographies have been popular from time im-
memorial, the aim of biography has changed considerably in the past two thousand years. Few books have
been read more than Plutarch's *Lives;* few books have
been as influential in stirring their readers' imagination.
Yet Plutarch assuredly did not pursue the modern biographer's pretentious aim of recreating the whole living
personality of those he chose to write about. His purpose
was, aside from historical, purely didactic and moralistic.
The "noble Grecians and Romans" whose lives he wrote
and compared were to serve as examples—guiding or
warning, as the case might be; his book was a school of
virtue. To be sure, Plutarch often sketches in, with brief
and bold strokes, some private characteristics and idio-
syncracies of his heroes; but essentially it is with their
public character, their relationship to society, their public achievement that he is concerned—and this concern is
made evident by the fact that his heroes all are public
figures in the strictest sense: monarchs, generals, law-
givers, statesmen. Not one philosopher, not one poet or

artist or scientist among them. Montaigne, in his essay *On the Education of Children,* emphasizes this didactic character of Plutarch: "In this association with men," he writes, "I mean to include, and foremost, those who live only in the memory of books. He (that is, the child) will associate, by means of histories, wth those great souls of the best ages. It is a vain study, if you will; but also, if you will, it is a study of inestimable value, and the only study, as Plato tells us, in which the Lace-daemonians kept a stake for themselves. What profit will he not gain in this field by reading the *Lives* of our Plutarch? But let my guide (that is, the teacher) remember the object of his task, and let him not impress on his pupil so much the date of the destruction of Carthage as the characters of Hannibal and Scipio, nor so much where Marcellus died as why his death there showed him unworthy of his duty. Let him be taught not so much the histories as how to judge them."

In our times, the emphasis in biographies has shifted from judging to understanding, and perhaps no man was more responsible for this shift than the one whom I just quoted. Montaigne never wrote a biography, not even an autobiography; but in the preface to his *Essays* he writes: "I want to be seen here in my simple, natural, ordinary fashion, without straining or artifice; for it is myself that I portray. My defects will here be read to the life, and also my natural form, as far as the respect for the public has allowed. Had I been placed among those nations which are said to live still in the sweet freedom of nature's first laws, I assure you I should very gladly have portrayed myself here entire and wholly naked." and Jean-Jacques Rousseau (who incidentally was skeptical of Montaigne's claims to frankness), went him one better: "This," he says of his *Confessions,* "is the only portrait of a man, painted ex-

actly after nature and in its entire truth, that has ever
existed and, in all likelihood, ever will exist." When Boswell, not long afterward, published his *Life of Dr.
Johnson,* he promised: "And he will be seen as he really
was." And he points out, with considerable justification,
that next to writing one's own life, there is no better qualification in a biographer than to have been intimately acquainted with his subject. To this effect
he quotes Dr. Johnson himself:

"But biography has often been allotted to writers, who
seem very little acquainted with the nature of their task,
or very negligent about the performance. They rarely
afford any other account than might be collected from
public papers, but imagine themselves writing a life,
when they exhibit a chronological series of actions or
preferments; and have so little regard to the manners or
behavior of their heroes, that more knowledge may be
gained of a man's real character, by a short conversation
with one of his servants, than from a fomal and studied
narrative, begun with his pedigree, and ended with his
funeral.

"There are indeed, some natural reasons why these
narratives are often written by such as were not likely to
give much instruction or delight, and why most accounts
of particular persons are barren and useless. If a life be
delayed until interest and envy are at an end, we may
hope for impartiality, but must expect little intelligence;
for the incidents which give excellence to biography are
of a volatile and evanescent kind, such as soon escape the
memory, and are rarely transmitted by tradition. We
know how few can portray a living acquaintance, except
by his most prominent and observable particularities,
and the grosser features of his mind; and it may easily be
imagined how much of this little knowledge may be
lost in imparting, and how soon a succession of copies

will lose all resemblance of the original."

To portray an entire man, to the life, with entire truth, as he really was — such has become the illusory, unattainable aim of the more ambitious biographer. Though illusory and unattainable, it may be more or less approximated. Of course, biographies still are and probably always will be written for other purposes too — to instruct, to inspire, to entertain, to gossip, or perhaps merely to display one's wit and art — and many such biographies are superior to the more searching kind. But if I am speaking of biography, what I mostly have in mind is the biography which tries to probe, to understand, and to make intelligible the mind and soul and heart of another human being.

The difficulty of the biographer's work begins with the choice of a subject. Choosing a subject for a biography is not entirely unlike choosing a wife, or rather, perhaps, a mistress. It may be a prearranged match: one's publisher suggests a subject, and one dutifully accepts it. In this case, the only choice to be made is whether to accept the commission or not. Or it may be love at first sight. An element of choice enters here: should one or should one not? Is it the right subject? Is it true love? Or else, the writer may simply feel an urge to write a biography and go on the prowl for his subject. In any one of these cases, the final result may turn out fortunate or unfortunate. One thing I regard as quite certain: that if you ask a biographer why he chose one subject rather than another, his answer is likely to be either just as woolly or just as disingenuous as the reply of a husband if asked why he married his wife rather than another. Motivations of this sort always are exceedingly complex, and though it may be convenient to have a pat answer ready, one should guard against ending up by believing it oneself. The biographer's motives for his choice are just as private as the husband's or the lover's.

If motivations are bound to remain obscure, qualifications are an entirely different matter. Ask yourself why Boswell chose to write the life of Dr. Johnson, and you will find that all the evident reasons pertain to his qualifications rather than his motives. "To write the Life of him who excelled all mankind in writing the lives of others" is the motive stated Boswell, and it may serve as an example of the woolly or disingenuous explanations I mentioned earlier; but when Boswell speaks of his qualifications to carry out that task, of the materials and the tools and the equipment that he could bring to it, then he is on solid ground. Yet the constellation of happy circumstances that presided over the writing of the *Life of Dr. Johnson* was so unique that one searches one's mind in vain to think of an even remotely comparable work in the world's literature. It is true, as both Johnson and Boswell contended, that to write another's life one should have known him intimately; but such acquaintance is hardly enough, nor is long association a guarantee of intimate knowledge: think of all the biographies that widows, sons, or servants have written of their late husbands, fathers, or masters, and how they merely prove that the writers have never known their subject at all and are merely intent on reviving or rearranging their own past.

Among possible subjects of biographies, let us then rule out personal acquaintance as being the exception rather than the rule in the literature.

If I dwell at such length on the choice of subject, it is because, in my opinion, all the rest depends and flows from it. Each subject is unique, and the methods to be applied to it vary with each case. Still, certain very broad categories can be established. Time, space, social station, are among the criteria. The greater the distance in time, space, and social station between the writer and his subject, the less of a chance there seems to be of creating illusion of direct contact and communication. If I were to write the life of Alexander the Great, what would I do? I can familiarize myself with all that has been written on Alexander by his contemporaries and in the age immediately following his; I can absorb all the new knowledge relevant to him that has been uncovered by historians and archaeologists in recent times. I can saturate myself with all that has been preserved, all that is known, of the civilization, the mores, the policies of his age, in Greece, in Egypt, in Persia, in India; I can follow him in his conquests, visit the places where he went, see the ruins of the cities he founded; I even can call to my aid modern psychology and medicine to help me understand and explain the violent contradictions and eccentricities in his character; I can think, feel, and live Alexander the Great for years—yet the best I can end up with is a reconstruction and reinterpretation, enlivened perhaps by my own intuitive imagination—an exercise in art and wit, in erudition and intuition. Not a mean accomplishment, but hardly a presentation of the entire man, portrayed to nature. Why? Not only because it is rather difficult for someone living on the San Francisco Peninsula, surrounded by television antennae, electronic plants, and barbecue pits, to seize the essence of the classical hero par excellence, but even more so because there is not a single personal document Alexander has left us. Indirect information and Sherlock-Holmesian detection cannot substitute for personal communication. The personal document, through which a human being can speak to us directly, across age and space, is all-important.

Still, even where personal documents abound there has to be some sympathy, some intelligence as it were, between the biographer and his subject. Not long ago a publisher proposed to me that I write a life of Napoleon, concentrating on his intimate personality. I know quite a bit about Napoleon—enough, in fact, to be quite sure that I don't like him, that I have a very personal dislike for him, despite all my respect and admiration. If I were to write such a book, it would not portray Napoleon at all; all it would do is expose at great length my puzzlement and ambivalence. His chief characteristic was to remain hidden. The best I could do would be to show, by personal documents left by him and those who knew him, how he wanted to appear at certain times and how others saw him. It would be a compilation of documents, a biography of sorts, but not the kind of thing we are talking about.

Who, then, is a proper subject for biography? We might start at the opposite end, and ask the question, Who is not? If the aim of biography is not to portray greatness or genius—qualities that usually remove the subject far from the writer's range—but rather to portray a whole person, then why not just take anybody, any average citizen, provided he has left a sufficient quantity of personal correspondence, receipted bills, tax declarations, and descendants, relatives, friends, and enemies who can be interviewed? Why not indeed? There are excellent reasons why not.

A few months ago an aged lady came to see me at my office at Stanford University Press, of which I am the editor, to consult me about a problem. For the past seventy years or so, she told me, she had preserved every piece of paper relating to her life — letters, receipted bills, cancelled checks, budget books, forms and documents of every description, including a complete documentary history of her 1927 Cadillac, every scrap of paper that can conceivably bear testimony to the fact that she had indeed existed at any particular point of time, even if her existence manifested itself in no more portentous a fashion than listing a number of personal items sent to be laundered. Feeling that this treasure should not be lost to posterity, she had hired a full-time secretary who for the past six months had spent eight hours a day sorting out and filing away her employer's life. Her question was, what to do with the documents. Now, there is no denying that if Madame de Staël, for instance, had left a similar collection, I would have found it useful and perhaps even fascinating while I was writing her life. But the lady in question was no Madame de Staël; all the documents of her life would have shown was that she had not lived; if a conflagration had wiped out both her and her files, nought would have been left. The remarkable thing about her was her maniacal intentness on proving to herself, for her entire long life, that she was living. This makes her interesting to some degree, more interesting than the millions who are not even aware of not living, but it hardly makes her a subject for a biography. It is true that nearly all of us, even the dullest and most insignificant, have our secret lives, our secret vices, heroisms, dreams, passions, fears, hatreds, and loves, but those do not appear in the documents we leave. Every person may be as interesting as the next, but to do justice to the secret personality of the average person requires a poet or a novelist rather than a biographer. By this I do not mean to say that only the great and the famous are fit subjects for biographies; it is entirely conceivable that some attic should conceal the letters and diaries of some entirely obscure man or woman, whose life was intense enough, and articulately enough expressed, to form the subject for an ideal biography. Unfortunately, only by chance can we stumble on such an attic.

I probably have already spent too much time on what

does and what does not constitute a promising subject. I should like to postulate now that it is best to choose a person who has made more of his life than the average person would; who has left a body of personal documents that enable us to feel in immediate contact with him; who has made enough of an impact on his contemporaries to enable us to see him through the eyes of others as well; who had some intellectual or creative capacities that set him apart from the commonplace; who lived at a time and in a society which is not too remote from those of the writer; and for whom the writer can experience a maximum of affinity — which does not necessarily mean approval. I said "he" — but of course it may as well be a "she." (Whether it is an advantage or a disadvantage for an author to write the life of a person of the opposite sex is a question that could be debated at some length, and the answer is likely to be, as answers to debatable questions so often are, "It all depends.")

Before I go any further, I think I ought to repeat here that the kind of biography I am speaking of is by no means the only kind that should be written. I am sure it is perfectly possible to write a life of Queen Nefertite that is a masterpiece of historical scholarship, literary craftsmanship, and imaginative reconstruction. But it would belong in the category of history rather than biography in the sense in which biography is understood by those who regard Boswell as their patron saint.

Once the biographer has chosen his subject, or decided that the subject suggested to him is indeed congenial to him, and once he has made at least a preliminary survey of the sources at his disposal, he must decide what form he will give his biography. The question of form may, at first glance, seem perfectly obvious. Do not all biographies begin with the birth and end with the death of their subject, with chapter divisions for various stages of development or episodes, and perhaps one or two chapters assessing the subject's accomplishments and character? Not necessarily. If the object is to present the whole person, rather than the whole life, then sometimes it may be preferable to select only a certain phase of the life—especially if that life is long and crowded—since such a limitation makes it possible to probe more deeply. If the biographee is a creative genius, the writer has other decisions to make which undoubtedly will affect the form of his book. Suppose he chooses to write a life of Beethoven. He may, with much justification, take the position that a discussion of Beethoven's works is beyond his scope; that even the creative process is essentially unknowable and therefore not to be touched upon; that an awareness of Beethoven's genius may be presupposed to exist in the reader. He may take all these things for granted and write only on Beethoven the man, dealing with his work only inasfar as Beethoven's working methods, successes and failures, hopes and struggles, are inextricably linked with it. That the work was music, in such a case, is almost irrelevant; he might as well have been a physicist. Surely such a biography will have quite a different form than one which, in every other chapter, analyzes his compositions and artistic development.

Other and equally important factors will determine the form. I cannot, of course, go into them, though I shall suggest some. What basic theme or themes are there in the biographee's life? What recurrent patterns? How much prominence should be given to those who played important parts in his life? What is the appropriate tone for its telling? To what degree should the documents be allowed to speak for themselves? The list is endless, and, of course not all the questions can be answered from the start. And, most emphatically, all the answers must flow

from the material itself rather than from any precon-
ceived notions of how biography ought to be written.

It may seem contradictory that if the aim is to present
the whole person true to nature, the methods to be used
in pursuit of this aim should all be concerned with se-
lection, limitation, arrangements of patterns, and other
artifices. Surely the patron saint, Boswell, was not concerned with such considerations but generally threw in
all he had, pell-mell and helter-skelter, in the order in
which it occurred to him, with only a rudimentary chronological skeleton, letting the personality of Dr. Johnson
merge spontaneously. He does, indeed, produce this impression, but I am certain that there is a great deal more
art than meets the eye—and this, of course, is the true
art—and that the pattern Boswell followed is by no
means haphazard. There can be no meaning without
form, nor can there be form without elimination of the
superfluous; nor, for that matter, is it possible to present
the whole person except as seen through another's tem-
perament, and this is why I remarked at the beginning
that the writing of biography was an impertinent and
hopeless enterprise, at least if it is undertaken in too
literal a spirit. The most the biographer can hope to ac-
complish is to learn from his failure while concealing it
from his readers.

Having chosen his subject and meditated upon it sufficiently to determine at least the general form of its presentation, the biographer faces the painful moment when
the actual work begins. (Just thinking and dreaming, it
is generally assumed, are not work.) What follows is
not so much the biographer at work as the biographer
as a drudge. First of all, he must read everything of
relevance to his subject that has been written, and he
will soon discover that more has been written than he
suspected and more is being written all the time. If he

knows a librarian who is helpful — and most librarians are helpful, provided they are treated right — this part of his labors can be greatly facilitated; even so, it is difficult to keep up with all the periodical literature, and there comes a point where even the most conscientious researcher should leave well enough alone.

I do not believe in taking extensive notes, and I believe still less in waiting to have finished taking notes before beginning to write. Coming down to the one concrete example I know best — namely myself writing the life of Madame de Staël — I cannot thank Providence enough for not having allowed me enough time to fall into either error. I read all the most important biographies and special studies of Mademe de Staël written before mine; I did not take a single note on anyone's ideas, opinions, interpretations, or theories about her; I took notes only of the other writers' sources and on their factual data, especially if the various writers were in conflict, and from these notes there emerged two very manageable files: one bearing purely on the chronology of events, the other on further sources to consult. If I had abstracted the earlier biographies, a gigantic file would have accumulated; I would have forgotten what was in the file; I would have had to read it and make notes on the notes in the file; I would have gone mad. And if I had waited until all my research was done before I began the writing, what I would have used for the writing would not have been the live raw material freshly remembered but mere lifeless abstracts, no longer directly experienced. True, the method of researching and writing concurrently has one great disadvantage: as one goes deeper into research one discovers numerous errors in what one has already written, and thus one is obliged to revise constantly as one goes along. This, however, it seems to me, is a price well worth paying.

Since Madame de Staël wrote voluminously, and much of her reputation and influence rests on her writings, I naturally also had to take the trouble to read the twenty odd volumes of her complete published works. It is a trouble some of the earlier biographers do not seem to have taken—or, if they took it, they apparently also took too many notes on what others had written on her writings. It is surprising how much one can learn if one's mind is not cluttered up with predigested judgments. I found a great deal in Madame de Staël's writings that reflected on herself and on her genius and that no one seems to have noticed before. The reason no one noticed it before was, undoubtedly, that at every period in history people see different things in the same books, provided they do not put on the blinkers of consecrated clichés about those books. To be sure, one also may miss seeing things that others have seen before, and to make sure that I had not missed anything I took the precaution, at a later stage in my labors, to reread once more the most important literary critics of Madame de Staël. I found I had missed a few things, and revised what I had written accordingly; but by and large I merely found myself in agreement with some of the critics and in disagreement with some others, and let the matter rest at that. I think it would be fair enough to formulate this general rule: If you are writing the life of a person who has left works behind, forget all you have read about those works and look at them with a completely fresh eye.

Another thing the biographer, if he is in the least conscientious, will discover is that none of his predecessors can be trusted. This discovery is made especially easily if a great deal of new documentary material has come to light since the earlier biographies were published. As

I went to the primary sources used by the earlier biographers and to those—published or unpublished—uncovered since their time, it became quite obvious that even the most elementary data had to be rechecked, at the very least. Yet there is a danger, in starting completely from scratch and using only primary sources, that new errors of commission or omission may creep in; thus I made it a point, wherever possible to check the data I had gleaned from my primary sources by comparing them with those given in the secondary ones. If there was a discrepancy, further investigation would reveal that either my predecessors had been mistaken, or that I had, or that the discrepancy could not be resolved at this time.

Perhaps the most difficult rule to follow in writing biography (or, for that matter, history) is never to take anything for granted, never to gloss over any difficulties, contradictions, or gaps, and never to cease asking oneself the same questions in every paragraph one writes: When? How? Where? Who? and so forth. If you yourself cannot completely visualize and make plausible the actions and facts you describe and assert, then you are not writing biography but merely rehashing earlier assertations. Yet the danger of wearying of these constant questions is very great, and the temptation to gloss over difficulties is at times irresistible. In everybody's life there are obscure and enigmatic phases; the biographer will at first try quite honestly to clarify them by diligent research. If, after a while, he discovers nothing that could shed light on them, he will don one of three things: he may explain the difficulty and admit his ignorance; or he may make a bold guess; or he may slide over the whole business by some devious trick or transition. (He may, of course, do all three things at the same time, thereby gaining the reputation for being con-

scientious and scholarly.) I have caught myself indul-
ging in this kind of glossing over on two rather important occassions in my biography of Madame de Staël,
and undoubtedly there are several others I am not
aware of yet. In both instances I was all the more inexcusable since I was perfectly aware that something was
amiss, and I was aware of this for the simple reason that
all the earlier biographers I consulted patently had in-
dulged in glossing over the same gaps in their information. In one of these instances I was rescued in
time from perpetuating my predecessors' blunder by
the fortuitous discovery of Madame de Staël's unpublished letters to the Vicomte de Narbonne — letters
which were kept, of all places, at the New York Public
Library. The discovery forced me to rewrite an entire
chapter. In the second instance, I did not learn in time
of the impending publication of another series of letters,
which shed an entirely new light on Madame de Staël's
relationship with Narbonne's successor in her favors,
Count Rigging. Such mishaps are no doubt inevitable,
but at least their number can be reduced by tire-
less questioning of every assertion one makes, no matter
how many authorities have made it before, and no matter how little important it may seem. The chances are
that behind every locked closet door there is a skeleton.

These no doubt are elementary rules to those trained
in historiography, but biographers not so trained tend
to be a slipshod lot.

I should like to emphasize that, in biographies such
negligences are important not so much because they
lead to an inaccurate presentation of facts or data,
which can be of interest only to specialists and ped-
ants, but because of the mental attitude which they
betray: lack of curiosity and lazy acceptance of ap-
pearances are inexcusable in a biographer.

The biographer's work is not limited, of course, to the hours during which he does his research and writing. Like the novelist, he must live with the characters of whom he writes almost every hour of the day and even, in a way, during his sleep. Otherwise their reality will always elude him. He must put himself in their place or, if he cannot do this, at least visualize and apprehend them from the outside, by constant analogy with his own entire experience of life and people. He can invent nothing, suppress nothing, he cannot rearrange the facts, and yet he must cast his unwieldy material into an organic shape much as the novelist creates an unvented universe, for only thus can he create an illusion of life and reality. I do not mean by this that the reader should not be kept aware that what he reads is fact and not fiction. Those biographers who try to make fact sound like fiction perversely deprive themselves of their chief dramatic asset in order to cater to a public that has been corrupted by historical novels. What I mean to say is that the end result of the biographer's labors should be an uncluttered and harmonious whole, the same as a good novel, and this result should be achieved without distortion of the given facts. As I remarked several times before, to write a good biography is pretty nearly an impossibility.

There is a belief among many biographers that to enhance the illusion of reality it is necessary to put in a vast quantity of background minutiae which supposedly "recreate a period." Historical novelists for the most part follow the same doctrine, which I quite frankly despise. A reasonable familiarity with the every-day way of life in the period of which he writes is, of course, essential in the biographer, but there is no need for him to unpack all his knowledge, even though the urge to do so is in the inverse ratio to the length of

time elapsed since its acquisition. The less self-con-
scious the writer is about the period of which he writes,
the more he will appear to be at home in it. His object
is to write about people and to understand them, not to
throw in treatises on costume, furniture styles, table manners, and the like. What interests us in people long dead
is not how they differed from us in externals but how we
recognize ourselves in them in essentials. I have read
many books—histories, biographies, historical fiction—of
which it has been said that they recreated a period. I
never found that I had become in the least acquainted
with the period from reading them, nor could I quite see
how the reviewers, unless they were Methuselahs, could
assert with such aplomb that an age long past had been
recreated to the life. I do not know what it was like to
live a century or two ago; I know only what it is like to
live now; and I defy anyone to claim anything else for
himself. If I want the age of Louis XIV to become alive
for me, I do not read someone's compendium of newly
acquired second-hand information: I read Saint-Simon.
In him, all is alive, and if he mentions anyone's dress or
table manners, he does so because he finds them peculiar or remarkable, not to inform his readers how people dressed and ate in his time. The biographer should
not turn into a social historian; though his work may
contain a great deal of social history, this element should
never be more than coincidental to his real business,
which is to write about people, very much the same
people under their dress as we are under ours.

After one has spent a great deal of time reading other
people's letters, diaries, and confessions, as the biographer must, one is likely to be oppressed by the same
melancholy thought that Benjamin Constant noted in
his diary after Madame de Staël had shown him the

letters and papers left by her parents: "What strikes
one most in these letters," he wrote, speaking of the
Neckers' correspondence with Gibbon, Voltaire, d'Al-
embert, Diderot, Buffon, and other greats of the 18th
century, "what strikes one most in these letters is the
uniform stream of life, the interest each one brings to it
in turn, and the profound silence that succeeds all this
busy monotony." Goethe had Mephistopheles make
pretty much the same reflection, at the death of Faust:

> Past! a stupid word.
> If past, then why?
> Past and pure Naught, complete monotony!
> What good for us, this endlessly creating,
> What is created then annihilating?
> "And now it's past!" Why read a page so twisted?
> 'Tis just the same as if it ne'er existed,
> Yet goes in circles round, as if it had, however:
> I'd rather choose, instead, the Void forever.

Perhaps so. And one asks oneself why one should go
to the bother of resuscitating people who are dead for
good. Perhaps the answer is that, in its modest way,
the biographers work is to undo, in as far as possible,
the devil's work: to assert the uniform stream of life
against the endless annihilation, and the intensity of
the moment against the busy monotony that immediately swallows it up. I really can see no other justification
for writing biography.

The Paradox of Fantasy

by

Robert Nathan

When Voltaire wrote Candide — in three days — he created a sensation in the world. At least, that is the impression I grew up with. And when Anatole France wrote Penguin Island, all of France — and a lot of other people — either hugged themselves for joy, or held forth indignantly over their soup. These books were satires—but they were also fantasies: works of imagination. No work of imagination today could hope to have such an effect.

There are many reasons for that. In the first place, one must simply admit that fantasy has gone out of fashion. I am not speaking of science fiction, or space travel — those books which today take the place of the Gothic romances of our ancestors . . . but of real, honest-to-goodness, old-fashioned fantasy — the thing that is almost true, but not really true at all, somewhere between a fairy tale and the Encyclopedia Britannica, somewhere between Cinderella and the Quantum Theory; and whose purpose is to surprise, and to delight.

I can remember, not so long ago, when books like The Wind In The Willows, or the Crock of Gold, were more or less required reading for the literate of almost any age beyond the elementary. And Gulliver, and Don Quixote. And then came Jurgen, and Lady Into Fox . . . I believe that Jurgen was one of the first books to be banned in Boston during what I would call my formative years. Naturally, it was a great success; not as great a success, of course, as *Peyton Place* but as I, say, times have changed. It's a lot harder to be banned today . . . People just don't seem to take fantasy seriously any more.

What made them lose their taste for it? Actually, some of the reasons are fairly obvious. The many wars, taxes, communism, juvenile delinquency, smog, the atom bomb, the scarcity of domestic servants . . . all these, plus a deepening distress, a growing anxiety — a tendency toward schizophrenia, and the loss of the sense of God in the world — have contributed to the realization that there is, after all, no escape, not even in the South Seas, and so things had better be faced. Today the reader wants to hear about life as it is lived— preferrably by his neighbor—complete with business problems, murder, or doings in the back seats of parked cars. Or else a bit of true history, a documentary — or a prescription for happiness, or the autobiography of an alcoholic. And for those who still want to escape into a happier world, there's the Sixty Four Thousand Dollar Question, and Queen For A Day.

It wasn't always that way. Thirty or forty years ago, a book like Leonard Wibberley's *The Mouse That Roared* would have become a little classic almost overnight. In those days people went to the book stores to buy imagination. It came separately wrapped, and brought enchantment with it.

But it rarely answered any day-to-day questions of living, or solved the servant problem, or taught parents how to bring up their children. As a matter of fact, I think that my Mother was always a little disappointed that I never learned to fly like Peter Pan.

My cook has a different approach to life. She is a horseplayer; she goes to the track every week-end, and bets on the races. Each week she loses her wages. But in her opinion, I am not a realist; I think, as she says, under a bush, which is her way of saying that I don't understand life, and that I ought to ride the buses as she does, and get to meet people. In her way, she is an intelligent woman. She said the same thing about Aldous Huxley when she listened to the radio broadcast of his *Brave New World*. What she likes in literature is for people to be married and to live happily ever after. She felt that *Brave New World* left them, as it were, hanging in space.

So much for the public — and for the low state of fantasy today. Dust has covered the laurels of Chesterton, Cabell, Blackwood, and Anatole France; James Stephens is all but forgotten; so is Dunsany and David Garnett; Kenneth Grahame and Milne — who, by the way, must be giving great delight to the angels — live at the far end of people's downward-looking noses.

Now then . . . what about the writer himself?—the obstinate fellow who lives under a bush, and must write his fantasies willy-nilly, whether anyone reads them or not?

There are not many of us left. As a matter of fact, you see before you, here on the platform, something practically extinct — like the whooping crane. Of course —

as I said before — I'm not talking about those writers (and very able men, too) who give us our science-fiction. That's another kind of writing altogether, and special, too, in its way. Its art is the art of strangeness and suspense; the reader says Impossible — and then proceeds to hang breathless on the outcome anyway.

But in fantasy — true fantasy, that is, as opposed to mad scientists and lost continents and visits to Mars — the reader must never be allowed to say Impossible. When a lady turns into a fox, it must appear to be, if not the most natural thing in the world, at least well within the possibilities. You will notice that I say possibilities, not probabilities. To the true creator anything is possible; he can create a flying Yorkshireman or a mousy Stuart Little with equal ease. Walt Disney has a word for it; he calls it "the-plausible-impossible." What he means is, that although the chances are overwhelmingly against it being true, it sounds real enough to fool you.

Fantasy can be satiric in intent, ironic in manner, tart or bland, savage or pitying; but above everything, it must sound plausible. I'd say of fantasy that it lays down a premise wholly untrue to our experience, accepts it as natural, and then builds an entirely human and homely story upon it ... which is to say, a story about homely and human characters, whether mice or men. In other words — accept the premise — and all the rest follows as naturally as summer. This is a definition which rules in the bitter political satire of Swift and the rueful irony of Kenneth Grahame, and rules out Tolkien's overpowering imagination. It is perhaps an arbitrary one; but I am trying to make a distinction between fantasy and a world that never was. *Alice in Wonderland* is a fantasy; *The Worm Ouroboros* is not. Like *The Lord of The Rings*, it is fascinating, unbelievably exciting, haunting ... but never believable. The witches and goblins of Ouroboros, the Balrog of the Ring, never lived on land or sea; the rabbit and the dormouse did.

Let me call this the first rule of fantasy: that the story itself, however unlikely, must never appear *im*-plausible. And as a second rule, I'd say that the writer must work with a loose elbow. By that I mean a free-striding, unfrightened imagination. And here is the first paradox: however loose and unshackled his imag-ination, it must at the same time be meticulously con-trolled. Take, for instance that wonderful moment in *The Mouse That Roared* when the army of the Duchy of Grand Fenwick marches off for war with the United States. It's a perfectly logical war; the duchy—all fifteen square miles of it—has it all figured out; it will lose the war, of course, and then, in due course, be rehabilitated by the United States to the tune of several million dol-lars, thus avoiding bankruptcy. (You see how logical a good fantasy has to be!) We see the army — all twenty of them—drawn up in review before the Grand Duchess ... the sun glinting and gleaming on the great eagle banner, on the swords and helmets of the three men-at-arms, on the armor of the twenty archers, clothed, as Mr. Wibberley says, "in mail shirts worn over leather jerkins and buff trunk hose, their six foot bows slung across their backs, their bucklers on their bare arms and their quivers bristling with arrows."

Notice the careful, almost meticulous description of these medieval bowmen. Mr. Wibberley's elbow never runs away with him. He continues:

"There was the beat of a kettle drum and the blowing of a trumpet and the group followed Tully out of the courtyard down the hill and over the bridge to the bor-der of the duchy. Little children lined the roads and

applauded. Old men and young women marched along-
side. They sang the ancient war song of Grand Fenwick, 'The Crooked Stick And the Gray Goose Wing.'
Some cried and some cheered and all felt very brave."

"Outside the border of the duchy the little army
changed into civilian clothing and caught the bus to
Marseilles."

This is fantasy in the great tradition, and at its best.
This is an instance of what I was talking about — the
free striding and at the same time controlled imagination which by its very earthiness, its common-sensible
restraint, adds such a human and irresistible gayety
to the whole. The army, dressed in its armor, marching
bravely through the duchy, to the plaudits of the pop-
ulace; and when they got to the border, they changed
into civilian clothes and took the bus to Marseilles.

It's a simple statement; but nothing could be
more revealing, and homely ... or perhaps it should
be the other way around—that nothing could be more
homely, and therefor more revealing.

It is these two things — the free-striding imagination,
plus the simple, homely statement, which help to make
fantasy believable. Or almost believable. And that's another thing about fantasy, which has a paradoxical
sound: it has to be believed — or almost believed.

And for that, the author has to believe it first. Unless
the author believes it — or almost believes it — no one
else will. The lady who turned into a fox was a very
real person to David Garnett; and he felt deeply for her
and for her husband, Mr. Tebrick. There will never be
in the world two people more real than King Pellinore
and good old Sir Grummore Grummursum, out of T. H.
White's wonderful fantasies ... as real as Piglet and Win-
nie The Pooh. Jennifer Lorn was as real as Washington
Square to Elinor Wylie; and Stephen Vincent Benet's

Doc Melhorne was an old friend of his. I really sailed with Hector Peckett across the George Washington Bridge and down through New Jersey and Pennsylvania. It was before the turnpikes, of course. And I knew Jennie Appleton very well — very well indeed. In fact — people used to go to the Metropolitan Museum in New York, and ask to see her portrait. After a while the museum bought the portrait, and hung it for a while. And about six months after *One More Spring* was published, some people actually did roast and eat a pigeon in Central Park — and some people lived in a tool shed.

Which brings me — in rather a small way — to another facet of the same subject: the curious — though occasional — moment when fantasy goes beyond what is known and touches some forgotten truth familiar, perhaps, to our ancestors, but unknown to our own doctors and philosophers. Do you remember in *Alice In Wonderland*, how Alice nibbles on a mushroom — the one that had the caterpillar on top — and first shrinks to a very small size, and then — nibbling on the other side — grows tremendously tall? Well — not very long ago I read an article in *Life Magazine* about mushrooms; how two very reputable and altogether respectable gentlemen had munched on some mushrooms in a Mexican Indian village, and had had incredible visions, very vast and grand. Lewis Carroll would have been surprised, but not astonished. I'm sure that the magic power of *his* mushroom didn't seem in the least unlikely to him; it was simply a matter of finding the right one.

Whoever writes — successfully — in fantasy must always believe what he is writing. He must be convinced that it happened that way; that it *had* to happen that way; or, if it didn't, that it might have — or if it mightn't, that it should have.

Let me tell you what Kenneth Grahame says about this, in the *Wind In The Willows*.

"Badger is asleep, Rat is counting over the spoils, and Mole is making Toad tell him all his adventures from beginning to end. The Mole was a good listener, and Toad, with no one to check his statements or to criticize in an unfriendly spirit, rather let himself go. Indeed, much that he related belonged more properly to the category of what-might-have-happened-had-I only-thought-of it-in-time instead of ten minutes afterwards. Those are always the best and raciest adventures; and why should they not be truly ours, as much as the somewhat inadequate things that really come off?

Well—why not? In its own way, it's a kind of positive thinking. A little extra dust on the moth's wing—a little extra fuzz on the peach.

When you believe it, it has a way of coming alive. I'm talking now of the writer, and what he writes. It's something he shares with children, who also create a world for themselves.

And that brings me to the final paradox of fantasy. In a good fantasy — which is a thoroughly unreal story — the characters have to be as real as your Aunt and Uncle or the girl next door. They have to be loved, and hated, and wept over and laughed at, just as though you knew them all intimately. And because they are apt to be very odd characters indeed—like a Mole, or a lady who turns into a fox—they don't get much help from anything or anybody except their author. And the author, being—as has been said—under a bush . . . has to work very hard to pull it off.

Fantasy is a great many things; it's part fairy tale and part satire and part comedy and part weeping for the world and part wanting to make a better one. But what-

ever else it is — or does — it must give the impression —
oh, more than the impression, the conviction — of being true, not in fact, but in essence.

Without that, you have nothing. The paradox is—lose
the truth from fantasy, and you lose the fantasy.

Robert Nathan

The Novelist as Historian

by

Frederick Shroyer

An historian may be defined as a scholar who explores
a plot of time which may lie between 9:00 A.M. of the
26th of October, 4004 B.C. — when, Jack Lightfoot solemnly assures us, the world was created — and yesterday. The goal of an historian is to learn all he can about
the area he has chosen and then to discover if there
are, any significant patterns in what he has found. If
there are, he affixes such findings to the factual material
he has amassed and contributes the total work to the
continuing record of man and his societies.

For these purposes, the historian consults all available
previously compiled materials that are pertinent to his
segment of study, and all available primary sources,
too. The kinds of matter he may consult include diaries,
letters, books, periodicals, artifacts, oral traditions,
Sears catalogs, and anything else that is germane.

When he has exhausted all these resources, he summarizes his findings, interprets them, and compiles a work of his own which then — and this is the nature of the historian's finest contribution — becomes a source for future historians.

Ideally, the historian begins his voyage of discovery with an acceptance of the obligation to follow where the facts he finds dictate. His professional oath demands that he not distort his material to fit any Procrustean bed built from the lumber of his wishes or of his previous convictions.

Not all historians have succeeded in remaining disinterested, of course. Cotton Mather has much to answer for, and we may hope that he rests penitently in his grave. And Parson Weems, too. Certainly Procopius and Virgil are highly suspect. And if it is not blasphemous to suggest it, it is probable that Arnold Toynbee has stretched history upon his metaphysical bed and done violence there with dogmatic stretchers and hatchets.

Undoubtedly complete objectivity is beyond the capabilities of all men, even the historian. He, like us all, is dismayed by the arrogant rebel fact that threatens to demolish his laboriously built structure. And the temptation is great to ignore it, or to shout it down. Nevertheless, the historian must try for objectivity, if he is worth the name, and he must seek to follow where truth dictates, no matter the direction of its path; even, in fact, if the destination lies at the end of a long, one-way road far from the warmth and the order of his own spiritual and national home.

Now everything that has been said about the historian applies to the novelist, for he, in his own approach to history — and what, one asks, can the novelist write about that is not history, or the stuff of history? — is

under the same obligation to follow where truth leads
him, and once there to survey the totality of his dis-
coveries, interpret it objectively, even though he may
not like the total that comes up, and then transmit in
his work what he conceives to be the truths he has
found. The novelist, like the historian, is often confronted by the rebel fact: the Romantic may be un-
happy to find that beneath the rose garden he portrays
is a blanket of compost; the Naturalist may be dismayed
to find a rose growing near the garbage pail he writes
about. But the novelist's obligation, like that of the historian, is evident. If he evades it, it is a criticism of the
novelist, not of the validity of the novel form.

The novelist differs superficially from the historian
in his apparent freedom to create imaginary characters and situations. But the difference is merely one of
the containers the historian and the novelist use. If I
may be permitted an unfortunate metaphor: the historian and the novelist may use different buckets, but
the water each contains — when both men are working
at their highest level — is drawn from the same well of
truth.

Again, the historian, though he uses the same general
body of source material as does the novelist, probably
finds its more objective, impersonal data to be of
greater value for his purpose than that which is more
ephemeral and personal. The novelist, on the other
hand, gravitates toward the area of social history for
his material. By social history I mean that concerned
with the more emotional and immediate characteristics of men and societies: what people wore, how they
made love and why they made love, what they laughed
at and what they hated, what they read and sang, what
they applauded and what they hissed. In short all the
things that were intimate and immediate to those the

novelist wishes to write about.

Let me approach this matter of the novelist's primary interests in another way. Today we live in an age when the very stratosphere above us glitters malignantly in the afterglow of atomic explosions; when men-made moons and missiles hurtle about the great globe itself. And yet, what are the most immediate concerns of those who live in this potentially catastrophic age? Even in this time of the trembling of nations? Salaries, I suspect, and love and taxes; baseball teams and television programs; sack dresses and sport cars; filter cigarettes and liquor; the Recession and car payments.

The historian will one day write about our age and he will cram his book with graphs and statistics and commentaries upon diplomatic notes and food production and consumption. For the historian occupies a high, removed niche on the side of mountains that brood imperturbably over vast areas of space and time. From his eyrie, the historian looks down with a cold eye upon men in masses; masses which flood as vast impersonal waters out of the dark horizon of the Beginning and disappear into that of the End. The historian's view is like that of a jet pilot's who sees the hundreds of cars on a freeway as one great, fused mechanical entity.

But the novelist, as he writes about our time, will continue to zoom in and focus upon the individual, for he knows — and sometime the historian doesn't — that in the entire universe there is only one thing that possesses an ultimate importance, and that is the individual. There is no removed niche for the novelist; he lives with men and he breathes their air; his mind merges with theirs; he *feels* the truths he finds among them, and he writes about them with joy and pain.

It has always been accepted that the novelist is often indebted to the historian; it is time, I think, that the historian became more aware of what the novelist can offer him. Of especial interest to the historian should be the novelist's ability to transmit superbly well the actual life stuff of an age or a people. The picture he creates is a living, closely seen one of the impact of social or broadly environmental forces upon his subjects. And, parenthetically, even a bad novel tells something about a kind of artist, and, if the book, though false, is accepted as true by his society, that fact reveals something very important about his society.

Further, the novelist insensibly reflects the mores of his own society, even though the subject matter of his novel be drawn from the past. Taking the Revolutionary War, as an example, one finds that it has often been the subject of historical novels. Around the turn of the century, Robert Chambers used it for his novels, and much later so did Howard Fast. Though the subject was the same, the books are vastly different. They both deserve to survive primarily because they tell us much that is valid and of historical value about the attitudes and the values *of the societies in which the authors lived,* though they contribute little of value to an understanding of the Revolutionary War. Out of the Chamber's book emerges the picture of a romantic, complacent and sentimental age; from Fast's, that of one characterized by uncertainty and feral struggles. Certainly there is something here that is worth the historian's attention.

In conclusion, I believe that both the historian and the novelist are motivated by the same high purpose: to discover what is true, to interpret it, and to contribute their works as other bricks to the ever growing wall of human knowledge and understanding.

Departing from the same destination, walking different paths at times — for the historian often gives the

highest rank to facts, while the novelist often believes
that truth is more important than facts — they yet remain within hailing distance as they progress. And if
they do not forget the nature of the mission to which
they have dedicated themselves, it is inevitable that
they will meet and exchange greetings at a common
destination: the high and hard-won place where truth
resides.

Unacknowledged Legislators and "Art Pour Art"

by

Kenneth Rexroth

The oldest and most popular subject of criticism is apparently the role of poetry and the place of the poet in society. The arguments of Plato and Aristotle are not early but late. Long before their day, on Egyptian papyrus and Babylonian clay tablet and in the Prophetic Books of the Bible the discussion was going on. As most of you may know, Plato had a very low opinion of poets. Isaiah had a very exalted one. From those days to the present the debate has continued.

In most cases the dispute has been so disputatious because so many of the participants have had a very inadequate idea of the nature of poetry, what it actually is, how it achieves its effects, what the arts do generally in and with society. I think the best way to start is naively and empirically to say that poetry is what poets write and poets are what the public generally

agrees are poets. In my time anthologists have included
everybody from Walter Pater to Vanzetti to Thomas
Wolfe amongst the poets, but actually very few people
would accept this judgment. Florid prose is not poetry;
in fact it is often very close to being the opposite of
poetry, rhetoric. The public seems to sense this. The
Dadaist poetry of Tristan Tzara is considered poetry,
even by people who neither like nor understand it. The
last page of the *Garden of Cyrus* of Sir Thomas Browne
or the sermons of Dante are beautiful rhetoric.

Let us start with a poet whose social responsibility
is not very manifest. He wrote during the few brief
years that the Roman Republic broke down once and
for all and Julius Caesar began the organization of the
Empire which came into full existence under Augustus,
a period of economic books and crises, of civil war and
the constant threat of social revolution both from the
upper and the lower classes. What have the poems of
Catullus to do with either Republic or Empire, with
the social collapse and conflict he saw about him? Is
there any evidence that he interfered in any way with
the society of his time? He wrote a lot of obscene and
abusive poems about Julius Caesar, Mammurra, Mentu-
lus, the millionaires of the "popular" cause. They were
personally motivated—he just didn't like them. Actually,
he seems to have belonged to their circle. He certainly
did not belong to the Senatorial party.

You could say that his poetry reflects passively the
first period of Roman decadence, the breakdown of the
caste system, the fall of the Republic, the spread of the
Empire far beyond the Italian peninsula, the looting
of the East, the emergence of the little circle of families
of tremendous wealth, the dying out of the old stern
ideal of Republican morality, the spread of a public and
a private morality through all classes much like that of

our own Hollywood or Cafe Society. It is always presumed that the Lesbia of his most passionate love poems was Clodia, one of the more notorious evil livers of all time, a multimillionaire courtesan like those who are always in our own newspapers. You could write a whole book like this and run it serially in *Pravda*, and you wouldn't have said anything important.

Nobody has ever valued Catullus for such things, from Clodia or Caesar to our own day. Men have read him all these years and will continue to read him for his pecularly exacerbated sensibility, the fine sharpness of his perception, the clarity and splendor of his language, and the heartbreaking pathos of — not the emotions he describes — but the actual emotional situations he recreates for us with such power, the drama of his own life in which he is able to involve us directly, as though it was our own.

This is certainly one of the things poetry does. It communicates the most intense experiences of very highly developed sensibilities. With whom does it communicate? Like any published utterance it communicates out into society with anyone who wants to be communicated with. The poet may envisage a specific audience, exquisites like himself, the proletariat, the "folk" — but actually he broadcasts and takes his chances with an audience.

Perhaps this is enough. As time goes on and the poem is absorbed by more and more people, it performs historically and socially the function of a symbolic criticism of values. It widens and deepens and sharpens the sensibility, and overcomes that dullness to significant experience that the Jesuits used to call "invincible ignorance." People are by and large routinized in their lives. A great many of our responses to experience are necessarily dulled. If to a certain extent they weren't,

we'd all suffer from nervous breakdowns and die of high
blood pressure at the age of twenty. The organism has
to protect itself. It cannot be completely raw.

What the arts do, and particularly what the most
highly organized art of speech does is to develop and
refine this very rawness and make it selective. Poetry
increases and guides our awareness to immediate experience and to the generalizations which can be made
from immediate experience. It organizes sensibility so
that it is not wasted. Unorganized sensibility is simply
irritability. If every sense impression, every emotion,
every response was as acute as it could be, we would
soon go to pieces. The arts build in us scales and hier-
archies of response.

As acuteness grows and becomes more organized in
the individual and in society as a whole — in the separate individuals who make up the abstraction "society
as a whole," it reorganizes and restates the general
value judgments of the society. We become more clearly aware of what is good and bad, interesting and dull,
beautiful and ugly, lovable and mean. Experience thus
comes to have greater scope, greater depth, greater intensity. Many activities of man do this—but it is specifically, primarily, the function of poetry.

Whatever else the arts do, and amongst them the art
of poetry, this is the simplest and most obvious thing.
If we stick to this we push aside a great deal of aesthetic argument. Is art — or poetry — communication
or construction? Criticism in the recent past has held
that the arts were largely construction, and that it was
the architectonics of the construction which provided
the criteria of judgment. All the arts were assimilated
to the canons of architecture and music. Of course the
answer to this is that Chartres or the Parthenon are not
purely construction. All great architecture, like all mu-

sic, is very definitely a kind of communication. The Parthenon says something, something quite different from what Santa Sophia says centuries later. This should be self-evident — San Vitale, Saint Front, Albi, Lincoln Cathedral, Richardson's Trinity, the U.N. Building — these are overpowering acts of communication, each widely different from the rest.

Purposive construction of any kind is a species of communication, just as any kind of communication must be structured. I cannot get paid for this lecture by babbling to you incoherently.

From the opposite aesthetic direction there has come in recent years in the art of painting especially, and to a lesser degree in poetry and music, the exploitation of what is called "the art of random occasion." People spill paint on canvas, ink their shoes and walk on paper, stare at a glittering point and write down their "free associations." Now the actual purpose of such activity is to show the kind of communication that emerges under the guidance of the sensibility and taste of the artist even out of the manipulation of accident. After all, nothing looks so much like a Jackson Pollock as another Jackson Pollock. This can be said of the work of all the abstract expressionists. As painting has exploited more and more the manipulation of random occasion, the more personal the paintings have become. I am not arguing about the ultimate value of Rothko, or Still, or Motherwell. I do not as a matter of fact think this is the very highest kind of painting. I am simply pointing out that any familiarity with it reveals how strongly personal, how individually communicative it is.

Is it that when you have a minimum of active construction and a maximum of chance and "inspiration" the unconscious mind operates to reveal the artist more intimately? I think not. The poetry of Paul Valery and

T. S. Eliot is presented as rigorously constructed, un-emotional, impersonal — "like the Parthenon." Like the Parthenon it turns out to be intensely personal. At the first glance at the page, Pope seems to be the most for-mal of poets. The sentences unroll in strict balance and antithesis, the carefully scanned couplets line up on the page with the caesura, the slight pause in the line, al-ways exactly in the middle. He is the perfect example of absolute obedience to eighteenth century French aesthetic theories. But what happens when you pay at-tention to the poetry? There emerges a tortured neurotic, shivering with a kind of exquisite irritability, one of the most personal utterances in literature. T. S. Eliot has told us all so many times that he has no emo-tion, that he never writes of personal experience. The truth is that his poetry is so personal that you can re-construct his whole inner life, his whole personal his-tory from it. It is as embarrassingly intimate as the revelations of the analyst's couch. Remember when he climbs the winding stair and looks out through the key-hole window and sees Spring on Westminster Place in St. Louis, and the flowering bushes, and all the agony of childhood? Valery too says there is no emotion, no "expression, no personality, no direct communication in his work. It is just architecture and music. And then in *The Marine Cemetery*, he cries out, "Ah, Zenon! Cruel Zenon d'Elee!" and the pathos of this man caught in the trap of his own gospel of implacable order over-whelms you, the torture of this mind hiding behind its formalism is almost more than you can bear.

In poetry, as in all the arts, both the constructive and communicative aspects are tremendously raised in power, but they do not differ in kind from ordinary speech. Only the aesthetician who brings to the arts considerations from elsewhere in philosophy, from ontology or epistemology, can postulate a different realm of being with its own kind of communication in poetry. Hector with his wife and child, Piccarda's speech to Dante, the ghost of Hamlet's father, these are all, however exalted, in the same world as "please pass the butter." Furthermore, medieval and "vulgar" aesthetics are perfectly right when they speak, as Plato and Aristotle did, of the Art of Cooking, or the Art of the Saddler. The only difference in the Fine Arts is that they are finer — and they communicate more, and more importantly. Albi Cathedral is the sum total of the work of its bricklayers as well as the plans of its architect. As construction the difference is simply one of degree. There is no sure point at which you can say, "Beyond is Fine Art." Instead in the constructive activities of men you have a continuum, growing in refinement, intensity, scope, depth and splendor. Here Thomas Aquinas and his modern followers are right.

Furthermore, certain works of art in recent years have taught us that you can apprehend even the simplest speech or simplest plastic arrangement, or, to take somebody like Webern, even a fugue on two notes, with the intensity of the artistic experience if you want to compel yourself to do it. Yoga and other mystical gymnastics of the attention have always done this. You all know the modern photographs of hopscotch squares in sidewalks, torn signboards, broken windows, piles of lumber and similar things. What the photographer is doing is focusing attention on something that was not actually structured in the first place. It is the attention which creates the structure. You can train yourself to see the clouds of Tiepolo, the mists and mountains of Sesshu in any waterstained ceiling.

Gertrude Stein did this with words. You say poetry is different, disinterested and structured. It is not the

the same kind of thing as "Please pass the butter," which is a simple imperative. But Gertrude Stein showed, among other things, that if you focus your attention on "Please pass the butter," and put it through enough permutations and combinations it begins to take on a kind of glow, the splendor of what is called an "aesthetic object" and passes over into abstract, architectonic poetry. This is a trick of the manipulation of attention. Pages and pages of Gertrude Stein are put together out of the most trivial speech, broken up and used "architecturally" to the point that ordinary meaning disappears, not from the sentences, but from the very words themselves, and a new, rather low-grade but also rather uncanny kind of meaning emerges. I happen to think that her work was valuable. It makes interesting reading for a while, but it is, by and large, a failure, because it lacks enough significant contrast to engage the attention for long. Besides, her interests, her conclusions about life, her ideas about most anything, are so terribly pedestrian.

To get back: What kind of communication are we dealing with in the arts? So much of our dispute about what poetry does, about what happens between poet and hearer or reader is due to old unsolved questions about the nature of knowledge and the nature of communication. This whole body of argument is peculiar to the Western world during the last three hundred years. The philosopher I. A. Richards once wrote a book, *Mencius on the Mind*, all about how the classical Chinese philosophers spent a great deal of time discussing epistemology, the problems of knowledge and communication. It is a very ingenious book, but it is untrue. What we call the epistemological dilemmas of modern thought have never existed for anybody except Western man. The whole problem of knowledge and communication never bothered other people in other civilizations. We forget that to a very large degree it does not bother the bulk of the people of Western civilization either. The epistemological problem arose as in Europe and America human relationships became increasingly abstract, and the relation of men to their work became more remote. Six men who have worked together to build a boat or a house with their own hands do not doubt its existence.

As human beings grow more remote from one another, they become more like things than persons to each other. As this happens the individual becomes remote from, *loses*, himself. First alienation from comradeship in the struggle with nature, then alienation from each other, finally self-alienation. A great deal of our communication is not with persons at all. It might just as well be a machine to which we say "Pass the butter." What we want is the butter. It is this which people mean when they say the communication of the arts is of a different kind. But this is not communication at all, it is verbal manipulation of the world of things. "Reification" an American philosopher once called it. The arts presume to speak directly from person to person, each polarity, the person at each end of the communication fully realized. The speech of poetry is from me to you, transfigured by the overcoming of all thingness —reification—in the relationship. So speech approaches in poetry both the directness and the impact of the unlimited potential of act. A love peom is an act of communication of love, like a kiss. The poem of contempt and satire is like a punch in the nose. The work of art has about it an immediacy of experience of the sort that many people never manage in their daily lives. At the same time it has an illimitable character. Speech between you and me is focused, but spreads off indef-

initely and immeasurably. What is communicated is
self to self — whole "universes of discourse." When we
deal with others as instruments, as machines of our desires, we as well as they are essentially passive and limited to the end in view. My relationship to a horse is
more active than my relationship to a car. Something
happens but it is outside of us. In the arts — and ideally in much other communication, the relationship is
not only active, it is the highest form of activity. Noth-
thing happens. Not outside in the world. Everything is
as it was before. We react to things, we respond to persons. In the arts we respond to the living communication of a person, no matter how long gone the artist
may be. In a sense, out into unlimited time and space,
say from the studio of an Egyptian sculptor, the artist
is speaking, alive, to us, person to living person. Of
course it is this which is the subject of the great poems
by Horace, Shakespeare, and Gautier: "No *thing* will
outlive the living word."

No thing happens. What changes is the sensibility.
It deepens, widens, becomes more intense and complex,
in the interchange between person and person. If, historically, this is a cumulative change, it is a very slight
one. There is no evidence that Picasso has "progressed"
beyond the paintings of the cave men of Altimira, or
that Sappho is less than Christina Rossetti. Progress
takes place in the world considered as an instrument.
And even here it is questionable if tools, means of production, which irrevocably separate man from man represent progress or decadence. I think the arts do progress, but they progress in their means, in their own instruments and in a slow growth towards more wide-
spread purity, that is, lack of adulteration with just
this reification. Of course, from the very beginning —
Sappho, the songs of the *Shi Ching*, this purity exists.

And the tone changes. Each age has its specific sonor-
ity, its response to its time. (The politician cannot understand this. For him all persons are things. So the
lyric folk songs of the Chinese *Book of Odes*, the *Shi
Ching*, were "interpreted" by the followers of Confucius
as versified political homilies.)

Often the poet, let along his audience, is not very
clear about what he is doing. Consider how certain
key poets in the European tradition have lifted up and
crystallized and illuminated the whole thought of their
epoch. This is particularly true of Baudelaire. Sometime ago I said in an article in the *Nation*, "Baudelaire
was the greatest poet of the capitalist epoch. Does anybody dispute this?" Well, nobody wrote any letters.
Yet Baudelaire had all sorts of idiotic ideas about why
and how he wrote. But more than any other poet for
two hundred years he communicated. He defined and
gave expression to all the dilemmas of modern man,
caught in the cruel dynamic of an acquisitive and continually disintegrating society, a society which had suddenly abandoned satisfactions which went back to the
beginning of human communities in the Neolithic Age.
Baudelaire, at first sight, painted the entire portrait of
modern man, urban and self-alienated. He speaks directly to each of us like a twin brother. And yet Baudelaire was hardly aware of the magnitude of his accomplishment — he had such foolish ideas when he tried to
explain himself.

Blake, in so many superficial ways, inanimate reification ways, the very antithesis of Baudelaire, plays a similar role in the founding of the modern sensibility in
English. He saw the whole picture of the oncoming
nineteenth century civilization with its dark Satanic
mills. He wanted none of it, but he came to grips with
it. It is very pertinent that for most tastes Blake's most

powerful wrestling with his time and the future occurs in his lyrics, not in his *Prophetic Books* where he presumes to deal with such matters explicitly, or at least allegorically. This is true of Burns, a specifically Jacobin poet — a professional revolutionary in a sense. He takes a simple Scotch folksong and ever so slightly alters its hackneyed lines with the slightest shading and change of emphasis. A whole new realm of values opens up. He does this more successfully in his lyrics in my opinion than in his long satires, admirable as those are.

The outstanding example of this social-historical role of the poet is Dryden. From the Puritan republic of Cromwell to the Roman Catholic despotism of James II, Dryden changed with the politics of his day. Each time he wrote a long poem to justify himself. It would be easy to dismiss this as time serving, but careful reading of the poems themselves carries the conviction of Dryden's sincerity. Although he became progressively more reactionary, the whole structure of his thought as he hammered it out in a new kind of verse and a new attitude towards reality presages the oncoming secular, republican, rationalist eighteenth century. Out of Dryden you can deduce Gibbon or Voltaire, but you cannot even imagine Cardinal Newman. Dryden himself, of course, was completely unaware of this.

So programmatic poets do not, by and large, even propaganda poet thinks of men as things and of poetry as an instrument for their manipulation. Again, consciously tendencious poets are crippled by their "message" and tend to be just that much less effective. Milton presumed to speak for the new era of Protestant middle-class republicanism. Yet his poetry is technically reactionary and looks backward to the Renaissance and even the late Middle Ages. The person we meet in Milton would have been happier in the court of that Henry VIII he despised, or of Lorenzo de Medici a century or more before him. Who speaks for France of the first half of the nineteenth century, Lamartine? Beranger? Or Baudelaire? We do not read Shelley for his dreary rehash of the woodenly inhuman and humorless ideas of Godwin but for the developing sensibility of the oncoming century which he shares with Keats. This is his unacknowledged legislation.

It so happens that until modern times few poets were "pure poets" in George Moore's sense — completely disinterested in anything but personal communication. Most poetry in the Western world is more or less corrupted with rhetoric and manipulation . . . with program and exposition, and the actual poetry, the living speech of person to person has been a by-product. The felicities of Dante are such by-products, of an embittered politician rewarding his friends and punishing his enemies and preaching an already outworn philosophy and cosmology and an ugly, vindictive and cruel religion. I think Dante was much more interested in putting the "other side" in various disagreeable pits of Hell than he was in the magnificent images of the gate and the first level of Hell or in the glory of Piccarda's speech. For this reason, although passages of Dante are amongst the very greatest in all literature, he is not so great a poet as Homer or Sappho or Tu Fu. The greatest poetry cannot redeem an obnoxious creed and an unpleasant disposition.

How few poets have this purity! Horace, Catullus, Sappho, Meleager, Asclepiades, Chaucer, medieval lyricists, Shakespeare in his songs, Burns, Marvell, Landor, Blake, Li Po, Tu Fu, *The Song of Songs*, the list could be prolonged, but not very far. A poet like Tu Fu has a purity, a directness and a simplicity — presents himself immediately as a person in total commun-

ication — in a way so few Western poets do. And yet,
even here this purity is partly a matter of perspective.
Tu Fu never forgot his role as a court official, a censor.
Even after he was fired and the T'ang court was de-
moralized and exiled, he went right on "admonishing
the Emperor." Much of this, couched in symbols of natural occurrence, simply goes by the average reader.

However, there are rare instances where the "message," the expository occasion that floats as it were the
the poetic accomplishment, is itself so profound, so deep,
an utterance of a fully realized person that it augments
the poetry and raises it to the highest level. This is certainly true of Homer as it is just as certainly not true of
Dante or Milton. As you read the *Iliad* and *Odyssey*,
the sublimity of the conception rises slowly through the
sublimity of the language. An old man, blind now, who
has known all the courts and ships and men and women
of the Eastern Mediterranean, tells you, with all the
conviction of total personal involvement in his speech —
"The universe and its parts, the great forces of Nature,
fire, sun, sky and storm, earth and procreation, viewed
as persons are frivolous and dangerous, from the point of
view of men often malicious, and always unpredictable.
The thing that endures, that gives value to life, is comradeship, loyalty, bravery, magnanimity, love, the relations of men in direct communication with each other,
personally, as persons, committed to each other. From
nowhere else."

The great Chinese poets say the same thing, except
that they make no moral judgment of the universe. They
have no gods to fight against. Man and his virtues are
a part of the universe, like falling water and standing
stone and drifting mist.

Make Yourself at Home

by

Harold Gilliam

You go along in the normal uneventful routine of life
from week to week and month to month and then you
happen to pick up a book that opens your eyes to some
new aspect of life and things are never quite the same
again. You see and feel and think differently.

This experience can happen to a thoughtful person
at any time, but it is particularly likely to occur during
adolescence, a time when the human psyche seems especially susceptible to new revelations. It happened to
me as a teen-ager, shortly after my first visit to Yosemite.
When I got home I walked to the local library and
asked about books on that area. The librarian gave me
John Muir's THE MOUNTAINS OF CALIFORNIA,
and I was so fascinated by it that I almost memorized it.
My mountain experience took on intense new meaning.
I began to understand the significance of what I had

seen. My eyes were opened to some of the processes that created the world around us and that continue daily in countless new acts of creation.

One of the long-term results of that awareness was the writing of my own book, SAN FRANCISCO BAY, in which I tried to deal with some of those processes as they developed in my immediate area. I owe an inexpressible debt of thanks not only to the great naturalist himself but to the anonymous librarian who first placed his book in my hands.

In view of such an experience, it is perhaps understandable that I have some strong biases in favor of regional literature. I believe that the development of a vigorous regional American literature is of surpassing importance not only to the individual who wants to cultivate an awareness of the world immediately around him but to the growth and development of this nation — particularly in its relations with the rest of the world at this point in history.

My title is from a book review by San Francisco poet Kenneth Rexroth published in the New York Times Book Review, October 27, 1958.

> It is ... identification with one's physical, historical, social, background that in the highest sense of the word, makes one a cultured man. You can know all about what Henry James really meant, or the art of the fugue, but if you are not at home in the world under your feet and before your eyes, you are actually uncivilized ... There are too many homeless people in America, many, perhaps most of them, with well-shined shoes. Make yourself at home. It is not just good for you, it's a pleasure.

Reading—or writing—regional literature is a process of making yourself at home.

There are a good many misconceptions about the nature of regional literature. In explaining what I mean by the term, I hope I will be forgiven for using, as an example, my own experience in writing SAN FRANCISCO BAY. I do so because it is the most convenient example and the only one I am fully qualified to discuss. I hope, however, that as I recount some of my experiences in writing about my own region, the reader will be applying what I am saying to his own region and visualizing similar ways in which his area has been or could be written about. Then we'll try to draw some conclusions about regional writing in general.

A number of people, in learning that I was writing a book about San Francisco Bay, assumed that I was doing a history of the Bay Area. I think this assumption betrays a certain conventional and rather old-fashioned way of looking at things. We assume too often that all the important things happened a long time ago. Actually the present is as full of importance and excitement as the past. History is but one phase of regional literature. It is a very important phase, but as long as we think of regional literature as history only, it will never achieve its full development.

I also had a hard time convincing people that I was not writing about the cities around the bay; I was writing about the bay itself — the water and things directly connected with it. Scientific writing aside, it is only recently that writing about inanimate things has come to be recognized as being as important as writing about people.

I would like to describe my experience in writing my book in terms of the education I received in the process. I learned, for example, that San Francisco Bay is a relatively young feature of the landscape, geologically speaking. The basin now occupied by the bay was a river valley not so long ago, and the Golden Gate was carved by the river — the combined waters of the Sacramento and San Joaquin — as the Coast Range rose in its path. At the end of the last Ice Age, when the great glaciers began to melt, their waters flowed to the ocean in such volume that all the seas of the earth began to overflow. As the ocean rose outside the Golden Gate, it flooded in through the channel carved by the river, inundated the river valley and created San Francisco Bay, which achieved something like its present shape only about 12,000 years ago — a mere moment ago when you think in terms of millions of years. Swimmers who wonder why the bay is so cold have their answer: it's melted ice.

During my research I found that although most historians name Portola as the bay's discoverer, there is considerable evidence to indicate that the bay may have been discovered nearly 200 years earlier by an Englishman. Francis Drake is known to have landed in 1579 at some natural harbor on the Northern California coast, but documents of his voyage do not make clear where it was. There are some intriguing clues to the mystery, including the famous brass plate which Drake inscribed, claiming this land in the name of Queen Elizabeth. The plate, which chemists believe to be authentic, was discovered on the shores of San Francisco Bay by a picnicker in 1936. Shortly afterward, another man claimed that he had found the same plate earlier on the shores of Drake's Bay, (30 miles north of the Golden Gate) and had discarded it near the point where the picnicker had found it. Partisans of San Francisco Bay refused to believe his story, but the argument was back where it started. Anyone is free to consider the clues and formulate his own theory.

I discovered that although most of the San Francisco Bay is less than 15 feet deep, the powerful currents have carved out some deep channels in its floor. On an average ebb tide, the waters flowing out the Golden Gate are equal in volume to seven rivers the size of the Mississippi. On an extreme ebb, one third of the bay will flow out the Gate — a volume equal to fourteen Mississippis. As a result of these mighty torrents, a channel 300 feet deep has been carved at the narrows of the Gate, and half a mile west the bay reaches its greatest depth at 382 feet, sufficient to swallow a 30-story building.

I learned that 40% of the freighters sailing through the Golden Gate fly the flags of foreign nations, Norway in the lead. The Bay Area's biggest customer is Japan; its most valuable cargo is coffee. One out of 12 cups of coffee consumed anywhere in the world is made from coffee beans shipped in through the Golden Gate and treated in San Francisco..

I learned that suicides go off the Golden Gate Bridge at the rate of about eight a year and are travelling 80 miles an hour by the time they reach the water. Only one person has survived the fall — a girl in her early twenties who said she never intended to jump but was walking across the bridge, happened to look down, was attracted by the fascination of height, and found herself involuntarily climbing over the rail. She was pulled out of the water badly injured but made a complete recovery.

I became aware of a fantastic range of life in the bay. Some one once pulled out an octopus with an eight-foot spread, and an 18-foot shark once got fouled up in the shipyard at Hunters Point. The electric ray — a cousin of the sting ray — can send out a jolt of electricity

strong enough to knock a man off his feet, and a
strange fish called the midshipman has a row of light
organs capable of creating enough illumination to enable you to read a newspaper— if you can work out
some way to keep the paper dry. A fisherman one time
hauled in a giant sturgeon weighing 1300 pounds, and
the largest creature of any kind ever found here was a
whale which washed up on a beach at Land's End and
weighed an estimated 60 tons.

I learned that the famous ship *Rio de Janeiro,* which
sunk in the Golden Gate in 1901 with the loss of 130
lives, was rumored to have had a treasure on board
and that the rumor was probably true. Several generations of diveers have failed to locate the hulk of the
Rio and she's still out there someplace on the bottom of
the bay. Her treasure, estimated at anywhere from
$75,000 to $3,000,000, belongs to anyone who can find
it.

An even more valuable treasure is the bay's salt. The
Leslie Salt plant around the southern edges of the bay
is the largest solar evaporation plant in the world, and
supplies 80% of the salt used in the West.

I learned that the Reber Plan for the reconstruction
of the bay so interested members of Congress that they
voted a multimillion-dollar survey of the bay to determine, among other things, whether the plan would
work. John Reber's idea involves the construction of
earth-fill dams across the bay to save most of the tremendous volume of water that flows into the bay from
the river and goes to waste out the Golden Gate. The
dams would also provide highway and rail transporta-
tion across the bay. As part of the authorized survey,
the Army Engineers have built in Sausalito an acre-
sized concrete scale model of the bay on which the
tides flow just as they do in the bay itself. The Reber

Plan will be constructed on the model to determine its feasibility.

In my research on the bay's islands, I learned that Alcatraz has not always been "escape-proof." A number of escapes occurred during the days when it was an army prison. On one occasion four prisoners who worked in the offices forged some documents recommending their own release and slipped the documents into the mail to Washington, where they so impressed the prison authorities that the papers were approved and returned to the warden at Alcatraz. He was surprised at the order, but did his duty and put the amazed prisoners on the boat to San Francisco, where they walked free.

I learned that the construction of the Golden Gate Bridge was an epic struggle of men against the sea, that storms off the ocean several times wrecked the preliminary works and forced the engineers to start over each time with new strategy. In order to cope with the fierce weather at the strait, the bridge was built with extreme flexibility—to roll with the punches. The deck was designed to be able to sway 28 feet in either direction under the impact of hurricane-force winds roaring through the Gate. The twin towers of the structure are so far apart that they must lean slightly away from each other in order to compensate for the curvature of the earth between them, and the distance of the deck from the water may vary as much as 25 feet under different conditions of weather, load, and tides. When the *Queen Elizabeth* entered the bay during World War II, she cleared the deck by just two feet.

I learned that the fog which sweeps through the Golden Gate and covers the bay a good part of the time during the summer is caused in part by the same force that makes the water circle to the right as it runs out the bathtub drain. The rotation of the earth causes anything in the northern hemisphere which moves freely to circle to the right. As wind tends to blow from a cool to a warm area, during the summer the winds from the cool Pacific blow toward the warm continent. As they do so, they are deflected rightward by the rotation of the earth and by the time they reach California are blowing down the coast.

These winds push the surface ocean currents along beneath them. This ocean current, moving down the coast, also veers to the right, which means that it veers offshore. To replace it, new water must well up from the bottom. This water from the sunless depths is very cold creating an icy streak along the Northern California coast all summer. The ocean winds, striking this frigid surface, are themselves cooled off. As their temperature drops, the moisture in them condenses in the same way that the moisture condenses on the outside of a glass of water. But the moisture of these winds hangs in the air, creating the great bank of summer fog that frequently blankets the Northern California coast. (The sheltered coast of Southern California is more often fog-free.)

As the Golden Gate is the only sea-level break in the Coast Range, the coastal fog pours through the Gate in a great flowing flood of vaporous air, creating fantastic fog-forms: fog-billows, fog-cascades over the adjoining hills, fog-falls down leeside cliffs, fog-domes over the islands of the bay.

The "tides" of fog rise and fall, ebb and flow, in cycles similar to those of the tides beneath it. In fact the advances and retreats of the fog can be described as the result of a battle between the cool air of the ocean and the warm air of the interior valleys, with San Francisco Bay as the principal battlefield. Thus the bay influences the weather not only in the immediate area but inland throughout California's great Central Valley — an area as large as all New England.

I learned, finally, that the processes which created this bay are still in operation, changing it continually. For example, as the sea level continues to rise with the melting of the polar ice cap, the bay is growing ever larger. If the process continues until all the ice is melted, the sea level will rise about another 150 feet. San Francisco will be a cluster of islands formed by the tops of its hills, and most of its neighboring cities will be at the bottom of the bay. There is no immediate emergency, however; this process will take place, if at all, only in another several thousand years. On the other hand, the great ice sheets may form again, causing the sea level to fall. The bay will then run out the Golden Gate, leaving a great expanse of dry land for the development of the bay's cities. Chambers of commerce, please note.

So much for San Francisco Bay. I have gone into some detail on this subject in order to illustrate the fact that regional writing is not necessarily confined to history but can deal with many other significant aspects of a region. Of course there are many other types of regional writing; novels, poetry, short stories can all be regional and contribute to identification with one's environment.

In the past few years there has been a reawakening of interest in the natural world around us. It is once again possible to have an interest in nature without being considered odd or old-fashioned, a "nature boy" or a "bird-watcher" in the derogatory sense. Probably Rachel Carson's magnificent book The Sea Around Us began this trend in literature; magazine articles, books, and anthologies of nature writing have become increasingly popular. Growing numbers of people are finding that an interest in nature is not only a fascinating hobby but contributes immeasurably to mental health and well-being in these anxious times. To know something about the natural facts of the world you live in—the rocks and land forms, the winds and waters, the trees and plants and animals—gives you a sense of being at home in a region in the same way that knowing the people of an area gives you a sense of being at home in that community.

John Muir, even though he was alone much of the time, was at home in the wildest of wildernesses — not only in the Sierra but amid the glaciers of Alaska or the jungles of the tropics — because he could read the landscape like a book and felt a sense of wonder and a sense of discovery every time he found something new. To be genuinely at home in the natural world is to contact the root sources of life and achieve a strong sense of spiritual invigoration.

This sense of being at home in the place where you live is particularly valuable in our age of anxiety. The confusion and uncertainty of these times gives us an urgent need for roots in a region or community. As traditional standards and conventions decay, the individual faces the need of making contact with things that are basic and elemental. Far more than in a time of security, he needs to face the ultimate issues of life and death, to define his own convictions, his own goals and purposes, his own relationship to the world around him and to whatever spiritual principles he can find there. Many a person who knows and feels at home in the natural world will testify that the best means of contact with these ultimate issues is a walk in the woods or a stroll on an uninhabited beach or a hike on a mountain or even simply a knowledgeable look at the sky overhead.

Contact with ultimate issues is facilitated not only by a more-than-nodding acquaintance with the world of nature but also by an understanding of the man-made processes of our environment, particularly those processes with which we have immediate experience and the thousands of human actions, both routine and creative, which are involved in getting us fed and clothed and housed and educated and entertained. A grasp of these matters is essential to the process of becoming "at home in the world under your feet and before your eyes."

The development of a regional literature dealing with these subjects is vitally important not only to the individual seeking orientation in a confusing world but, as I indicated at the beginning, to the American nation at this point in history. Just as the individual needs to be particularly aware of his goals in a confusing time, so does a nation. Surely no one would deny that we are living in an era when in order to survive we must have a clear idea of our purposes as a people. The great question Americans must answer in this revolutionary age is not a question concerning the Soviet Union or the Middle East or the H-bomb. It is a question concerning America. Before we can work out specific answers to the world's problems, we must first ask ourselves what our purposes are. We must settle the problem of our own identity. Are we a prosperous, self-satisfied people, interested only in keeping things as they are in the world, in maintaining the status quo so that we may enjoy our wealth undisturbed? Or are we still a young, vigorous nation of doers and changers, of movers and shakers, advocates of new plans and new ideas, remaking the world every generation?

I don't know the answer. I hope, of course, that the answer is the latter. But I do know that much of our current literature is literature of defeat and despair or literature of neurotic escape and irresponsibility, such as that produced by the so-called Beat Generation. Some of this literature is technically of high quality, and a writer should write what he feels and believes, whatever it may be. But I believe we also need a literature mirroring the healthy, vital qualities in American life. Literature helps shape a people's image of their own identity. And the crisis of our times is a crisis of the American identity.

All this may seem to be a long way from my subject of regional writing, but actually it is highly relevant. The question of the American identity is not going to be answered in pious platitudes about democracy and freedom. It is only going to be answered in specific terms — at the grass roots level, at the regional and local level. It is going to be answered in terms of specific people doing specific things. An American literature giving a picture of the vital, creative aspects in American life is not going to be written primarily in New York or Washington. It is going to be written, if at all, in your community and mine and hundreds of others. It is going to be in some significant degree regional writing. It is going to concern, among other things, people making creative responses to challenges. It will enable the reader to establish identification with his environment, both natural and social.

I can anticipate some objections. Someone may say that it is all very well to talk about regional writing in San Francisco, which is one of the most colorful places in the world, but that most communities lack literary interest. They have no great harbor, no procession of ships from around the world, no exotic animal life, no Golden Gate Bridge. My answer would be that every community has a history of some sort; every community has a geologic background; it has trees and plants and some extraordinary people — all of which can be fascinating to the residents of the area.

Another objection might be that although writing about such an area would be of interest to the people who live there, it would not attract a sufficiently wide public to make books on the region commercially profitable for a publisher. For one thing, however, I suspect that there are much greater local markets for such literature than have been explored. Even more important is the fact that some of the greatest possibilities for regional writing are in the non-commercial fields. One of the "source books" I used in writing about the island of Belevedere in San Francisco Bay was a small mimeographed volume written by the sixth-grade class in the school there. The students talked to old-timers, examined old documents and maps, and wrote an excellent short history of the area. Why not similar publications on various aspects of a community by classes in various subjects? A science class might develop a publication on the trees of the area, or the weather or the water supply or the geologic background. A high-school economics class might do a volume on the business and industry; an English class could write biographies of prominent residents or make a study of the origins of local place names.

Aside from the schools, every community has residents who write or aspire to write and could be instrumental in developing local materials. Obviously there would be little or no financial reward in most cases, but the satisfaction of having a book in the local library or bookstore—even though it were only a mimeographed pamphlet—would certainly be an inducement to those who write as a hobby. Possibly P-TA's, local businessmen, chambers of commerce and similar organizations could be interested in sponsoring such projects and might even raise a few dollars to have the material printed in some attractive format. The possibilities are unlimited.

All this of course would be done on a very modest scale. This type of publication is not going to shake the world or create immortal literature. But if such projects, either amateur or professional, were developed in dozens or hundreds of communities, they could make a very substantial contribution to the growth of regional writing that would help the American people develop a vivid image of themselves and their country. The question of the American identity — like the question each individual must answer about his own identity and purposes—can best be answered by people who have the perspective and vision that comes from being at home in their environment, people who cultivate knowledge of the world around them and their relationship to it.

To sum up: we need a regional literature. We need writers who can help us establish our roots in the natural environment and who can express the native vigor and creative energies of the American people in the middle of the twentieth century. We need to be aware of our own identity as a people in such a way that we can come before the world as the bearers of a revolutionary tradition, with new perspectives, new affirmations, new plans and blueprints to meet the challenge of this revolutionary age. We need individuals who have made contact with the elements of existence and feel at home on their own part of the earth.

"There are too many homeless people in America," said Mr. Rexroth, "most of them with well-shined shoes . . . Make yourself at home. It's not just good for you; it's a pleasure."

About "Exodus"

by

Leon Uris

One thing that will get a writer into an argument is to tell him what an easy racket he has. He gets up by mid-afternoon and enjoys the luxury of being his own boss in totum. I learned early in the writing game that in order to be a good writer, you've got to be a bad boss. Self-discipline and stamina are the two major arms in a writer's arsenal.

As librarians you all have wondered at one time or another, I'm sure, where all the ideas came from in the vast stacks of books that surround you. Where are all the men and women whose dreams were so numerous, whose desire was so great.

Because Hollywood seems to be a symbol of all that is wicked, let me tell you a Hollywood story about a writer who got his ideas from clipping newspapers apart and turning them into elaborate filing systems. Whenever this writer wanted an idea, he would go to his files and look under either murders or ship sinkings or sex crimes or spectacular personal achievements. His well of ideas seemed inexhaustible. Moreover, he was so alert with the morning paper that anything that looked the least bit promising was immediately registered in the story department under his name. I'll call this fellow Jones.

Jones worked at Paramount when I was there. It wasn't long before I heard of his legend. It became the ambition of us all to beat Jones to a story. One day I was in my office and instead of writing, I was listening to a world series game. A fellow by the name of Lew Burdette had won two games against the Yankees and was on the way to scoring the prodigious feat of whipping them three times in a row. As the game wore on, I thought to myself . . . this time I'm going to get Jones. Burdette won the game and as the last pitch was thrown, I picked up the phone and called the story editor and told him I wanted to register a title. He answered . . . "If it's the Burdette story, Jones called this morning when he found out Burdette was pitching and said; 'if he wins the game, the story is mine.'"

Jones' method is, of course, the one way to get an idea, and I may add; the bad way. For myself, I must become personally involved in what I write. Ideas are slow in birth.

I feel that there has been a swing away from the great literature of the twenties and thirties where writers were driven by the social injustices of their times. I feel further that the great books which have been passed down to us have chronicled the times in which the writer lived. Today we find most writers of the World War II era and post-war era serving personal manias rather than causes. They psychoanalyze themselves between covers of a book; air their beefs against society; expose

their own maladjustments and pawn it off as fiction.
These men are plain and simply, beatniks, and beatniks
are bums, and bums don't write good books.

Battle Cry, my first novel, was a Horatio Alger story.
I came home from work late at night, wrote in an attic
and, after striving all my life, became an overnight
success. I was faced with the dilemma of having written
a smash first best-seller and wondered where does one
go after climbing Everest on his first try. This is an awe-
some problem that many writers of a big first novel
never solve.

I decided to mark time, to branch out to Hollywood
and learn screenwriting despite the frowns of my publisher.

I've got another Hollywood story to tell you. When
working on the screenplay, I went back to New York on
business and was to be interviewed by a very famous
lady interviewer; whom I'll call Miss Smith. When I
got to my hotel the phone rang and Miss Smith on the
other end of the line greeted me and asked me what
we would talk about on her program the next day. And
she continued . . . "Tell me about Hollywood." I told
her the screen play is rounding out nicely, and she in-
quired if they weren't ruining the book as they always
do. I advised her they weren't and there are many cases
of the screenplay being better than the book. She
switched to wild Hollywood parties. I said the wildest
one I had seen was a May Day dance at the children's
school. She kept up with variations on the same theme
until I became quite aggravated. I said: "Madam . . . .
I wrote *Battle Cry* in an attic with bills hanging over
my head, sick children and a sick wife. It took me three
years of working at a regular job during the day and
writing all night and 16 to 18 hours on my days off. Well
. . . I've come to Hollywood and I have a lovely air

conditioned office, a secretary, an enormous salary and they send me all over the world to do my research. I like Hollywood."

There was a dead silence on the other end of the line and she finally said a startled . . . "Well! You can't tell that to my listeners . . . they won't believe you anyhow."

So, I won't tell you about Hollywood.

After my screenplay, I had to at last come face to face with a second novel. It was a terrorizing aspect. I chose for my theme a small and insignificant event and constructed a spy chase. But it was in writing this book, which is famous for the fact that no one has ever heard of it, that I really learned the craft of writing. The putting of one word after another in the creation of a story with which I had not personally lived. We all have one *Battle Cry* in us. It was a book that was in me all the time. This second novel was an experience that separates the men from the boys.

Rod Serling, a very talented TV writer once said that no matter how glamorous a writer's office is, when he puts the seat of the pants to the seat of the chair it becomes a small dark room. And that is how I learned to write . . . in a small dark room; by hanging in there and vowing that either I was going to whip this second novel, or it was going to whip me.

It was after this second novel that I felt I had acquired the craft to go on and top Battle Cry.

My first awakening to a Jewish conscience came a decade ago during the Arab-Israel War. I have no formal Jewish education and I don't speak Hebrew. I have not been confirmed into my faith and, moreover, my wife is not Jewish. Yet, I had to come face to face with a problem that many Jewish writers write about. There came that day of reckoning when I had to say . . . "I am a Jew and what am I going to do about it and how am

I going to live with it."

With a great deal of sadness I must say that foremost among the beatnik writers are those Jewish authors who make caricatures of the Jewish people . . . the wily businessman, the brilliant doctor . . . the tortured son . . . the coward.

Although I was strange to Jewish life, I wanted to be proud of my people. I wanted to be able to write a book about Jews and be able to face a Jewish audience afterward.

And so . . . after a decade of incubation and development as a writer, I felt qualified in giving total commitment to a vast project.

I went into a crash program of research; of reading one to three books a day and went into a physical training program to withstand the rigors of strenuous travel.

As I moved my field of inquiry overseas I traveled fifty thousand miles in search of my story . . . to Iran, to Cyprus, to Italy, to Denmark and twelve thousand miles inside Israel itself; a country no larger than the State of Connecticut. I traveled by air, sea, car, jeep, camel, and by foot. I took fifteen hundred films, and a like number of interviews. I expended miles of recording tape and took hundreds of pages of notes.

I wanted to find the anatomy of a miracle; for when one speaks of Israel, they speak of miracles. I found that miracle makers were men with calloused hands. Miracles come from the same place good books come from. . . . hard work.

As this vast storehouse of material grew I grew somewhat confused. It reminds me of a story about a camel who was about to cross the Nile River. A scorpion came up to him and asked the camel to take him over the river on his hump as he was too small, and might drown. The camel said, "I know you scorpions. You'll bite me in the middle of the river and I'll die." The scorpion answered, "that's ridiculous. If I bite you and you die . . . I'll die too." Well, the camel thought it over, felt safe because it was logical, and said; "Hop on."

They got to the middle of the Nile and sure enough, the scorpion bit the camel. The camel turned around amazed and said, "What did you do that for." To which the scorpion merely shrugged and answered, "That's the Middle-East for you, brother."

Despite the amount of data collected and the impressive statistics of my research, what I was actually looking for came to me in slow, mysterious mosiacs. I wanted to write *Exodus*, not only for the Jewish people, but I wanted to reach beyond to the great American public and communicate a story of a people with whom they share the common bond of the Bible.

Perhaps I could best illustrate a piece of the mosaic by relating to you one of dozens of dramatic incidents. I was in the Negev Desert with a patrol of Israeli paratroopers. You'll see on my dust jacket picture on the back of the book I'm hanging onto a machine gun. This appears romantic, but the fact is it was 127° in the shade and if I were not holding on, I would have collapsed.

We passed through miles of slate fields which did not give life to so much as a blade of grass. It was the end of the earth . . . as bleak, as desolate as the face of the moon. Suddenly the patrol halted and the leader said we were going to take a break by a water well nearby. I thought the sun had gotten him. . . . I saw no well.

"This is the wilderness of Zin," he said, "and we know that Moses stopped at this same well on the way to the Promised Land." Yes . . . the well was there and it still had water in it.

My wife joined me in Israel; closing our home and bringing three children and a dog half way around the world. It was here, with these mysterious mosaics unfolding before me every day that I began work on Exodus.

I had no more than gotten my feet wet when the Sinai campaign broke out and I was compelled to evacuate my family on one hour's notice. This was a disastrous thing for us. It meant losing what was left of our money and most likely any chance to start the book for several years while I recouped through screenplays.

As they flew off under an umbrella of protecting American jet planes for parts unknown, I went into the Sinai as a correspondent. I may add; I was probably the shortest lived correspondent on record. I filed three stories and the war was over. However; the title . . . foreign correspondent looks good on a book jacket.

When I saw the wreckage of what was once the Egyptian Army, I asked one Israeli commander what the hurry was. He answered that they were looking for Mt. Sinai to give the commandments back to God . . . it's caused the Jews enough trouble.

The days after Sinai were black indeed for me. I didn't know where my family was . . . or if *Exodus* were doomed to be one of those unwritten books. One day I called upon my friend, Sholem Asch. I moaned out all my troubles in a frank quest for sympathy. Instead; the old man looked me in the eyes with a face not unlike an ancient prophet. "What kind of a writer are you?" he asked. And I realized that for fifty years of his professional life he had struggled for recognition among his own people. I felt a bit ashamed. "And," with the simplicity of a prophet he said . . . "someone has to write this book . . . you know what must be done."

The year of 1957 was spent writing and rewriting the million and a half words that ended the quarter million you now see between the covers of *Exodus*. I am asked . . . was it worth it . . . would I do it again? I say. . . . . I would never do a book with less preparation.

I think . . . of all the rewards that *Exodus* has brought me, the greatest came in a simple statement by a friend who told me that he was sorry when he finished the book . . . . sorry because he was not Jewish.

There are too many walls in this world, and not enough bridges. As the Aso-African people emerge from centuries of darkness little Israel is destined to lead the greatest renaissance the world has ever seen. It is her destiny now as it has always been, for Israel is a bridge from darkness to light.

I thank you.

Why Read Books

by

Leonard Wibberley

I have been very kindly invited by Miss Boaz to talk on the subject of "Why read books" with permission to touch also upon the fields of libraries, literature and philosophy. And I feel that with this amount of scope I should be able to come up with something startling if not useful.

First of all I think we might address ourselves to the main head — why read books — and in order to get into that we come up against the question of who does read books anyway.

During the past week I have been moving house and I had some very fine statistics available establishing beyond a quibble that we in the United States read fewer books per head of population than the British, French, Belgians, and the inhabitants of the Republic of Iceland,whom we have only recently come to think of as being literate in any degree at all. I am sorry to have lost those statistics, they were authoritative, exact, interesting and totally misleading. They created the impression that Americans do little or no reading at all, and that there is no great segment of the American population which are devoted lovers of books.

That, of course, is nonsense. There are Americans who read books consistently and have created a great demand for them. Without this segment of the population, constantly demanding not only new books but also copies of books published previously, most book publishers would be broke. These literate Americans, far ahead of the rest of us in their book reading, what we might call the avant guarde or perhaps the intelligentsia of the land, are of course juveniles. We of the writing profession — librarians, publishers, booksellers and authors owe them a great debt. Far from being juvenile delinquents, they are juvenile benefactors. Far from being a vicious population devoted to the smoking of marijuana and the robbing of liquor stores, they are the bright literary hope of our present days and of our future. We ought to pronounce a blessing upon them every night before going to bed.

I know what I am speaking of here for I myself write two kinds of books — books for juveniles (or young adults if you insist upon euphemism as is the modern social fashion) — and books for adults or older juveniles to carry out the figure to completion. I haven't had time to go fully into the figures but I believe that most of my juveniles have outsold my books for adults. I confidently expect that they will live longer and that their final sales tally will readily outstrip the totals for my adult novels. And I do believe that juveniles enjoy the books they read, I get quite a number of letters from them, and only recently received one from a boy in Chicago saying how much he had enjoyed a work of mine and asking whether I had written any other titles. I wrote that indeed I had, and sent him, for his pains a copy of one of my other books. This was immediately followed by identical letters from two other boys in Chicago (living on the same street) who said how much *they'd* enjoyed one of my books and asking whether I was the author of other titles. Complimentary copies are of course on their way to them. I am happy to encourage this kind of activity, not too far short of a sort of polite piracy, among young people. I was guilty of plenty of it in my youth.

There is only one flaw in this happy picture of juvenile literacy and I have made a practice of putting it strongly aside as springing perhaps from a measure of misanthropy in myself. That flaw is that perhaps the juvveniles do not really read the books. Perhaps adults, conscious of the fact that *they* should read books themselves, conscious that they are cultural sinners in that they do not do so, hope to mitigate their offence by buying books for their teenage friends . . . . . rather like a man preaching temperance over a quart of bourbon. This led to a further speculation that maybe adults do not like teenagers whom they regard as at least potentially delinquent if not actually delinquent, and to punish them for being teenagers they buy them books instead of do-it-yourself safe cracking kits on their birthdays.

But let us quickly agree that this is all misanthropy on my part, and that the largest books reading section of the American population, the true literati, are our teenagers. This presents a bright picture for the whole publishing industry for the future. For the habit of reading, acquired in youth, will certainly remain through adult life. I confidently predict a growth in book reading in the United States year after year until it will certainly be worth while for an author to consider giving up whatever employment he may rely upon for his food and rent and turn his energies exclusively to writing, as I have done myself.

But having examined the glorious example set us by youngsters more literate than their parents, let us consider for a minute whether *adults* do any worthwhile amount of book reading, or indeed whether they do any considerable amount of reading at all.

This brings us immediately to the survey previously mentioned which created the impression that Afghan riflemen in the Khyber pass are somewhat greater book readers than our own citizens catching the bus to Inglewood. Surveys such as this one however, ignore the fact that the United States produces some of the best magazines in the world (and some of the worst newspapers) and that general magazine circulations in this country far exceed those of other nations. So we are not at all a continent of illiterates. Indeed, we read voraciously. Considering the amount of reading which is done in this country, I sometimes wonder where we get the time for other cultural activities such as sipping cocktails, running off with each other's wives and occasional murder. But let's face it. We are not great book readers. My guess is that we never were, and my guess is also that neither were the European nations great devourers of books in previous generations. Comparative statistics are happily lacking and so I can elaborate on this point without fear of some literary mathematician popping up to prove me wrong. (It is an odd characteristic of our times how we think any discussion can be finally settled by quoting statistics, as if we were all machines, and figures added up were the measure of our minds and our feelings and our activities)

When Charles Dickens was writing his great social novels, he was writing for an illiterate England. When Thoreau was at Walden, compiling his journal, he wrote also for a largely illiterate America. Or to look at the other side of that coin, Thoreau and Dickens wrote for a comparatively small audience of highly educated readers, readers whose education was of the liberal rather than the technical sort, whose interest in man was not the parochial interest of the psychiatrist. These literate few were a book conscious people. They bought books as being the source of lifeblood for their minds. They bought and read them for intellectual stimulation and exercise. They were keenly interested in their own cultural growth, and would be as ashamed to admit that they had not read twenty novels in a year, as we would be to admit that we had had but twenty baths in a year. The emphasis is in the opposite direction today. A man who has taken a hundred baths a year but whose reading is confined to comic strips is an acceptable social figure. To digress for a moment, I recall at a certain local college overhearing a group of teachers discussing their summer vacations when they had gone visiting different parts of the world. One, whose journeys had taken him through the near and middle east, remarked that the further east he travelled, the worse the people smelled. What a sad comment that is, that people should be judged by body odor, as a dog judges another dog. I wonder whether this particular teacher, given the opportunity of a half hour's chat with Socrates, would first of all have demanded that that valiant rascal be taken out and thoroughly scrubbed. There was no running hot water in the house of Socrates, and frequent bathing in hot water, was looked upon quite rightly with suspicion. You will recall, of course, that Napoleon dated the decline of his mental faculties from the time he took to soaking in a hot tub.

Anyway, I think the point has been made that we are great readers of magazines and of newspapers, but not great readers of books, and this brings us at last (and properly by way of ancient Greece) to our real problem — why read books.

Is there, for instance, something about a book which makes it superior to a magazine? Might it not be held that a magazine offers a far greater variety of content than any one book and might it not be held that this diverse fare is better nutriment for the mind than the one major theme which a single novel is likely to contain?

Again, might it not be stated with confidence that magazines (which in this country have taken over the functions previously fulfilled by newspapers) present us with a great numer of factual articles about matters affecting our everyday living? Do they not then furnish the mind better than a book does? And the subscription to a magazine for a year is likely to be about the same as the purchase price of one novel. So again why read books?

The answer in my view lies in a variety of factors which examined singly may seem of small account, but taken together add up to an overwhelming argument in favor of book reading as the highest literary activity of any cultured society.

Let us look first of all at the permanence of books. Books are astoundingly durable. They have a quality of survival which is breathtaking. The other night for instance, as a result of reading a book, I went fishing with a man who died nearly three hundred years ago. His name was Izaak Walton. My son can go fishing with him also, after I am dead. And my son's son. And his son also. So that the pleasure of snatching a grasshopper up in an English meadow, casting it upon a hook into a quiet stream and listening at the same time to the gentle voice of Walton discoursing upon the merits of angling will persist through time as long as the English language — or any language — is read.

Here surely is a measure of immortality. I have spoken of Walton for the memory is fresh with me. But the same is true of all the writers of books of any merit — our own Thoreau, Emerson, Whitman, and so on through the list of authors of this nation and every nation. So that through books we can discuss with the minds of men whose bodies were dust two thousand years ago. The book is the true time machine. Books of today will inspire tears and laughter among people to be born a thousand years from now. One examines that thought with reverence, and one looks upon books properly as holy things. They are far holier, far more deserving of respect than a tomb, for they contain the essence of the dead man — his spirit, his mind, his imagination, his suffering, his sympathy, all as bright and flashing as the day he drew breath and walked among his fellows upon the earth.

But this raises the question of whether the same is not true of our magazine reading? Magazines are a comparatively new publishing venture — perhaps not much more than two centuries old. Will not some of our magazine writing live also, and is not magazine reading therefore the equal of book reading.

The answer, for me, is no. Magazines have a built in transitory nature. This has nothing to do with their paper binding and stapled leaves. It is a quality rather of their content. Think back to the last time that you examined an old magazine. How old it really was — not old in an interesting way but old in a dead way. How tawdry its stories, how inconsequential its articles. The weekly magazine dies in a week — it is a butterfly of publishing. The monthly magazine lives perhaps a little longer but it is dead in a year. Some special kinds of magazines have more permanence — and yet they died within our lifetime, and are of interest only for their quaintness and their peculiar mark of restricted viewpoint and mawkish manners.

Why? Why should this be? Why does the writing in the magazine die so fast, but the writing in a book — a good book — partake of immortality.

The answer is in part that magazines are largely printed to entertain and part of entertainment is the topicality — the up-to-dateness of the viewpoint. And nothing is deader than yesterdays's up to date point of view. It is quite as out of date as yesterday's fashions in women's wear.

That is one reason why magazine writing in my view is so short lived. Another reason is that the magazine writer writes for the magazine. The book writer writes for himself.

I want to dwell on that point to make it quite clear, for I regard it as important. If you want to sell a story to Collier's you have to read Collier's and study its content and find out what kind of story Colliers is buying. In other words you write for the editors of the magazine in the hopes of producing something which will please them, which will be similiar to the stuff they normally print and which has proved popular with their readers. It is tremendously difficult to do this and it calls for long study and much skill. It is financially rewarding, but it is not self expression. Rather it is the attempt to put into a story actions, chracters and plots which will please others then yourself — to please them is the first requirement. Far from this being self experssion magazine writing is a form of self denial. I deeply sympathise with those who are successful at it.

Now consider the approach of an author writing a book. By book I mean writing something in story form or some other suitable form, in which the story is secondary really to the theme which the story illustrates or brings subtly into focus. I do not mean the man who writes a detective story, or a Western story about the great American open spaces, or a bedroom story about the great American closed spaces.

The author does not first consider what kinds of books are published by what kinds of publishing houses. He does not, for instance, read all the current works on the Random House list and then try to produce something like them. He writes his book for no editor and indeed for no section of the reading public. He writes it for himself and then hopes that some publishing house will find it of merit with some possible sales value and will undertake to publish it.

Here then is the main difference between book writing and magazine writing — that the book as I have said before, contains the essence of a living man or some good part of that essence. The magazine contains only an example of writing skill designed to interest a particular editor who aims at interesting a particular set of readers. Tastes change and so most magazine writing becomes dated and dies. So do those books which have been written to meet a popular demand for lust, murder and gunfighting. But other books — real books which express the humanity of the author do not die for humanity does not change. We may look in our schooldays on the Odyssey as a mere adventure tale and a wildly improbable one at that. But as we mature we see that the travels of Ulysses are the travels of all men beset on every side by evil in all kinds of guises. So the

Odyssey never fails us, it is as fresh today as when it was first written by Homer and it will remain fresh as long as humanity remains human.

We might examine this matter of books versus magazines as living literature by inquiring into detail more closely. A great number of books to be sure are of something of the same nature as magazine writing. They *are* written for a particular market in the hope of making the best seller list. They *do* contain a mass of shallow but gaudy matter which it is hoped will have popular appeal. Some of them *do* make the best seller list. But how quickly they are exhausted — how old they become in a matter of a couple of years. Who reads many of the best sellers of 1950? Few of them have survived. Try it sometime as an experiment and you will wonder how so paltry a book could ever have achieved so wide a circulation.

Again there is the question whether all magazine literature dies in a comparatively short while — whether none of it has lived to form a part of the body of acceptable literature today. Well, some has survived — a very small amount compared with the great mass of the whole. Many of the essays from Addison's Spectator and Tatler are still current, reprinted in anthologies. If you read them you will find their major interest lies in the light they shed upon the curious and attractive atmosphere of 18th century England with its coffee houses and its quaint version of the war between the sexes. They do not provoke much deep thought. They amuse by giving us a window into the past, and they retain our interest because the English used has a certain grace not unlike the delicacy of a minuet.

Much of the sentiment is contrived, yet there is an occasional note struck which echoes readily across two centuries. In one essay of Steele's, I believe, musicians are admonished not to tap their heels to keep time during the playing of a number. That delights me, for I play a little music myself and note that the heel tapping tendencies of musicians are still strong. Again there are complaints about women's dress — always a point for superior discussion among men. So in these essays there are links with present times which have kept them alive.

Other essays have also survived from other periodicals. Swift's Drapier letters, for instance, though today they are of interest more to historians than the general reader. Swift's Modest Proposal for reducing poverty in Ireland by selling a hundred thousand plump Irish children a year as food to English gentlemen with jaded appetites. One claps with delight at this vigorous satire. Some of Robert Louis Stevenson's essays and those of Emerson have also survived after being published in periodicals. But as I have said, such survivals are few and it is noteworthy that they have survived in book form. The book in short is the lasting literature though let me emphasis that not all books are lasting literature.

So much time for why read books. If you wish to travel in the past, if you wish to visit Philadelphia at the time of the Revolutionary war, or Greece at the time of Plato, or Rome when Caesar pushed the boundaries of the empire over the Alps into Gaul, if you want to destroy the silence of the tombs you can only do so through books.

Let's take a look now at what kind of books are selling today and why I believe they are selling. This will give us a chance to get off into a little philosphy of a sort and perhaps give us a perspective on our times which we might otherwise miss.

Nothing is surer in the publishing business than that

at the present time two kinds of books have the greatest appeal. The foremost of these are those which have
a spiritual or high moral cast. The second are the how
to do it books — a phenomenon of the publishing business of some significance.

Why should these spiritual kind of books have such
a wide appeal today? Is it healthy that they should be
so popular? Or are we being seduced into accepting
a series of false values with the publishing business
playing the part of the long awaited anti-Christ? (I
have suspected for some time that when anti-Christ appears, he will be a publisher)

The greatest reason for the popularity of such books
in my view is that we have just gone through about
four decades of dwindling faith. Our scientific and
technical knowledge and ability is much increased, so
that compared with our grandfathers we have come to
think of ourselves as supermen. Side by side with this,
the work of Freud on the mind and Darwin on the body
— work ill-examined and scarcely understood — has produced a suspicion that all in humanity can be explained
in medical or psycho-medical or anthropological terms.
We destroyed the mystery of ourselves and when a man
is inclined to accept the fallacy that he understands all
about himself and his most secret desires are susceptible
of scientific explanation, he loses faith and belief. If
everything can be explained then nothing has to be believed and faith must dwindle. That is the road we have
walked along for some three generations though careful
to attend church with regularity out of a desire more to
please the neighbors than avoid offence to God.

Then we found that this was an empty way of life.
We made individually and collectively the discovery
that man cannot live by bread alone. There was in us
all a sense of vacuum and we could not go back to the

Bible because the geologists had explained that the earth is a lot older than the Bible allows and that it wasn't made in the way laid down in Genesis and furthermore God did not create Adam and Eve; that we done by the Missing Link, who for that work alone must surely be awarded the palm as the most talented creature to have trod the face of the earth.

Yet we needed something more than the assurances of the anthropologists and the psychiatrists and the psychologists and all that hellish crew who would divide us with their tests into alpha beta and gamma kinds of people — these monsters who pronounce all oak leaves alike, but have never stopped to consider that there is no single oak leaf in all the world precisely identical to any other oak leaf in all the world.

So what did we do? We turned back to our bible, but not the old Bible. We turned really to rewrites of the Bible and made these into best sellers for our hunger was and is very great. Take one book which has been a big best seller in this field — the Power of Positive Thinking. This is nothing more than a book-length extension of that single sentence in the New Testament which states that if you have faith as big as a grain of mustard seed you can move a mountain. Our grandfathers were quite familiar with this sentence and believed it and because they believed it, settled and built this continent. We had forgotten if, or if we remembered it at all, we didn't believe it. Now we get back our belief by reading a book in order to discover what our inferior grandfathers learned in a sentence.

Again, a recent best seller, especially popular with women was and still is Anne Morrow Lindbergh's "Gifts from the Sea". And this also is a book length extension of a few sentences from the New Testament — very beautiful sentences which are to be found in Matthew,

Chapter six.

"Consider the lilies of the field how they grow; they labor not neither do they spin; but I say to you that not even Solomon in all his glory was arrayed as one of these. Now if God so clothe the grass of the field which is today and tomorrow is cast into the oven, how much more you, o ye of little faith . . ."

So it goes on. We have made or are making the discovery that man is not explainable in terms of man. We cannot fully explain ourselves. There are parts of us — the most important parts of us — which escape all our methods. We are not our own designers and creators. We cannot find all the answers but must turn to that other Creator who alone possesses full knowledge.

I believe that this increase in the sales of the spiritual kind of book is a very healthy sign for us — a sign of maturity in this nation and if it is not abused promises a bright and healthy future.

Now the other kind of non-fiction books (we'll get to fiction in a minute) which are selling well. These are books concerned with our twentieth century hunger for knowledge. Again they show a healthy trend. Who would have thought that a book called "The Secret of the Hittites" would have been a best seller in this allegedly commercial nation? What kind of profit can a man make out of discovering the secret of the Hittites — presumably it has nothing whatever to do with removing facial blemishes or dressing the hair? No commercial profit at all. But there is a gain in the furniture of the mind, in the rounding of our thought and approach to life, in the perspective which we take upon ourselves which is well worth having. In short, we have filled our bellies with the produce of our factories and fields, no man need go hungry, no man lacks shelter. Famine is banished and disease retreats before medicine. We turn now to our minds and spirits and this turning is not merely one by college professors and scholars. It is a turning by the layman to new mental and spiritual activity. It is and I say this solemnly, the beginning of a second renaissance.

Think of that for a moment. The prosperity and resulting leisure brought to medieval Italy by the merchant bankers of the kind of the great Medici family produced the first renaissance with its miraculous effect upon mankind even to the present day. And here in this country now we have the same kind of prosperity and a far greater increase in leisure. Already there are the glimmerings of the dawn of a second renaissance which, if it continues and grows, will utterly eclipse the first. That century which produced the hydrogen bomb may well be hailed as the century which produced the greatest advance in culture and thought in the history of the western world. The tools are all at hand. Books, good books, are abundant. The literacy rate is at an all-time high. Men are not bedevilled by the struggle to feed and clothe themselves. These matters are taken care of almost automatically. There is a huge increase in our leisure and that increase will be greater as automation takes its proper place in our industrial lives. We are to be the first generation released from the bondage of the belly able without fear to turn ourselves to the explanation of the mind, to the reasons for man's existence and his motivations and what should be his objects. This has hardly been done since the days of the early Greek philosophers. The answer which we have now are the answers which they gave us two thousand and more years ago. It is time that we pressed further into the fields which they first explored.

There are signs that we are doing this. We in America have the Power of Positive Thinking and the gallant and agile French have, with their extentialism produced the Power of Negative Thinking. Between the two surely progress is to be confidently expected.

But what about our fiction — is there anything significant in what is selling well in this field. I believe there is. Our novelists today are concerned with the problem of the individual man. They have reversed that line of Donne which said that no man is an island unto himself. They are insisting that every man is an island unto himself. This, of course, is immaturity, the agony of the adolescent who finds the world impinges upon him cruelly and has not yet discovered that he is part of the world and has not stopped to reflect that though he has individuality and dignity he would be a monster if completely solitary.

This examination of the man as a solitary being stems I believe, from our century old love of self pity. We've had an orgy of it. We've wept our maudlin tears over our lost generations (how many lost generations did the hundred years war produce — lost and unsung but they did not pity themselves). Our typical war novel takes a young lieutenant or sergeants with a variety of personal fears and doubts and problems, caught in the hurricane of slaughter and pities him, pities him, pities him. The reader pitying him can pity himself and such books find a wide appeal through self-identification. The sergeant, as one astute commentator has pointed out never realizes, that he is in the war because he has a duty to perform; that the defense of his country and the principles for which his country stands are more important than him. He forgets if he ever realized it that he is a soldier and the noble job of the soldier is to give his life so that others may live in peace.

A good novel, though not quite a war novel, with

this solitary man theme is "The Man in the Grey Flannel Suit." Here is island-man — the unique product of the twentieth century — reduced to his final futility. He is so far removed in his work and his thinking from the mainstream of his times, from the prime sources of life and happiness, that he cannot even repair the crack in the plaster of his living room wall, nor fix up his garden. His true tragedy is that he has forgotten if indeed he has ever knew, how to grow grass. He is four layers removed from nature and his natural world is replaced by the artificiality of the mid-day luncheon cocktail, the ride to his suburban cell which he struggles to keep as well as the cells of his neighbors, and his struggle to find himself.

He can't find himself because he is too concerned with himself. He fathers a child in Italy but the Italian girl he took to bed was a sort of mother substitute for him — a comforter for this quite worthless and unmanly specimen.

What is significant to me about this book is that it made the best seller list and remains on the best seller list. In other words, hundreds of thousands of people have found an identify with this pitiful male object who certainly doesn't add up to anything approaching a man. That is the mark of our times — for the present. Unused to war, spoiled by a legacy of isolation, we go to war in a welter of self pity feeling ourselves abused. I do not like war. But I like less those who pity themselves because they must become soldiers. I abominate the mothers who soften their sons until even in manhood they remain babies. How different they are from those women of ancient Sparta who bade their sons return either with their shields (a sign that they had not run from battle) or dead upon them.

Still this, as I said, is merely our adolescence. We are

I believe likely to grow up emotionally, to tire of this island-man weeping softly to himself as he plucks the lint out of his navel, and find in the relationship between man and his fellows worthier material for our novelist.

I find the future bright and to sum up, I say that ahead of us lies a renaissance of unmatched brilliance, possible through our increased leisure, our increased literacy, our abundance of libraries and our abundance of books.

For myself as a writer, I look at the future and laugh with exultation, and go to my typewriter with zest and a high heart.